FEED THE FIRE!

FEED THE

FIRE!
Avoiding Clergy Burnout

Bruce G. Epperly *and*
Katherine Gould Epperly

THE PILGRIM PRESS
CLEVELAND

The Pilgrim Press, 700 Prospect Avenue, Cleveland, Ohio 44115-1100
thepilgrimpress.com
© 2008 by Bruce G. Epperly and Katherine Gould Epperly

Scripture quotations, unless otherwise noted, are from the New Revised Standard
Version of the Bible, © 1989 by the Division of Christian Education of the National
Council of Churches of Christ in the United States of America and are used by
permission. Changes have been made for inclusivity.

Printed in the United States of America on acid-free paper that contains
post-consumer fiber.

13   12   11   10   09   08   5   4   3   2   1

Library of Congress Cataloging-in-Publication Data

Epperly, Bruce Gordon.
    Feed the fire! : avoiding clergy burnout / Bruce G. Epperly and Katherine Gould
    Epperly.
        p. cm.
    ISBN 978-0-8298-1795-9 (alk. paper)
    1. Clergy—Job stress.   2. Burn out (Psychology)—Religious aspects—Christianity.
I. Epperly, Katherine Gould, 1950–   II. Title.
BV4398.E67 2008
253'.2—dc22   2008011409

CONTENTS

ACKNOWLEDGMENTS
A Word of Thanks

As we complete this book, we are on the eve of a new year. The new year is filled with promise and uncertainty in our own lives, mainstream Christianity, the nation, and the planet. Our only son Matthew is on verge of completing his final cycle of chemotherapy for germ cell cancer. We began this book looking forward to the celebration of his wedding and now conclude it while sharing the challenge of cancer. While the prognosis of a cure is good, we recognize that there are no absolute guarantees even as we surround him in God's healing light through prayer and healing touch. The United States of America seeks new presidential leadership to respond to issues of global warming, economic uncertainty, and war. The congregation we pastor, Disciples United Community Church, and the denominations with which it is affiliated, the United Church of Christ and the Christian Church (Disciples of Christ), look hopefully toward the future, despite the challenges of the present moment. In such a time as this, we are called to be flexible and visionary frontier thinkers. We are called to feed the fire of personal, relational, congregational, and global transformation so that the world might truly experience God's healing touch.

This book is the result not only of our unique partnership and synergy, but our relationships with pastors in Lancaster Theological Seminary's ministerial excellence groups, supported through the generosity of the Lilly Endowment, under the guidance of Craig Dykstra and John Wimmer, for which we give thanks. Bruce most especially thanks the participants of these colleague groups, whose giftedness and commitment give us hope for the future of the church. Bruce also thanks his colleagues on the faculty and staff at Lancaster Theological Seminary and is grateful for the support and leadership of President Riess Potterveld and Academic Dean Edwin David Aponte.[1]

We are also grateful to our congregation, Disciples United Community Church, a progressive open and affirming congregation, whose free spirit has encouraged us to express ourselves theologically and spiritually without apology and has enabled us to be our best in the practice of ministry.[2]

We also thank our parents, both living and deceased. Bruce is especially grateful for the encouragement he received from his father, Everett Epperly, that still lives on in his teaching, administration, and ministry. Bruce and Kate are particularly grateful for the ongoing personal support and inspiration of Kate's mother, Maxine, now in her ninth decade. We are blessed by the love that has emerged in our growing relationship with our son Matt and the growing circle of love embodied in his marriage with Ingrid and their intimately caring circle of friends.

A note about names: Most of the pastors whose stories we've told are currently congregational ministers. Accordingly, we have altered names, places, and genders, as well as created "composite" stories to reflect the joys and challenges of ministry today.

We conclude with a prayer for those who read this book. May you experience God's fire and warmth that gives guidance, endurance, energy, and inspiration so that you may be God's partner in healing the world and sharing Shalom.

ONE

BECOMING FIRE

The story is told of the encounter of a North African monk with his spiritual guide. Devoted and faithful to his vocation, Abbot Lot still desired a deeper relationship with God and so he sought the guidance of Abbot Joseph. "Father," he asked, "I have kept my little rule, and my little fast, my prayer, meditation, and contemplative silence; and according as I am able I strive to cleanse my heart of thoughts: now what more should I do?" In response, Abbot Joseph rose up from his chair and stretched out his hands to heaven, and his fingers became like lamps of fire. "Why not become changed into fire?"[1]

Become fire? A devoted minister comes to a wise spiritual director with a similar question. "I have dedicated my life to God, working tirelessly for the past ten years to enable this congregation to grow spiritually and reach out to the community. I've worked hard to be a good spouse and parent. I do my best to pray regularly and take care of myself. But still I struggle to

1

experience God as a living reality in my daily life. What more should I do?" In the spirit of Desert Father, the wise spiritual director responded, "Why not let yourself be so transformed by God's lively spirit that your life is aglow with God's brightness for all around to see?" Or in the words of Father Abbott, "Why not become changed into fire?"

Today's pastors face unprecedented challenges in ministry. Whether just out of seminary, in mid-career, or looking toward the horizon of retirement after four decades of faithful ministry, most pastors work hard and seek to respond ably to congregant needs. Week after week, they preach the gospel with fidelity and care, and often go straight from the pulpit to care for the infirm, the sick and the dying. Yet many of today's best pastors are near burnout, physically, emotionally, and spiritually. They still go about their tasks with grace and commitment and lead their congregations with integrity, but find themselves losing their focus and feeling fatigued as they race from one "urgent" task to another, finding little time or support for creative discernment about what is most important in life and ministry. They don't know how to set and keep priorities for their own health and well-being. The fiery vision that brought them to ministry is often eclipsed in the course of performing the day-to-day repetitive tasks of ministry.

Susan describes her condition with the word "brownout." The dedicated pastor of a 250-member congregation in a mid-Atlantic state, this single pastor in her thirties struggles to have any sort of life of her own apart from her pastoral role. "If I let it, this church will devour me body, mind, and spirit. This church is at a tipping point and needs all the attention I can give, if it is to move ahead in the next five years. I can't do enough, it seems, to move the church forward, and, yet, some days, I really don't know what to do. Should I devote more of my time to preaching or evangelism, to social involvement or pastoral care? And now the church is contemplating a building campaign and wants me to be the cheerleader. I don't know if I can make it through this next stage of our church's growth. I'm not sure I have the energy or vision to lead this congregation anymore. I barely have time to pray, exercise, or go to a movie with a friend."

Craig feels the same way about his life and ministry. The father of two young children, the spouse of an educator, and a veteran of ten years in ministry, this suburban pastor feels harried most of the time. "I just can't seem to catch up. Now that I've been here five years, the culture of the church is changing and it's really taking off. We're growing in numbers, giving is up, and our budget has increased by 25 percent. I should be happy, because this is how success is defined in ministry. But so are the demands, and it seems like no one is listening when I say I need help to lead this church, especially when I express the need for an associate minister or someone to do visitation with the senior adults. I love ministry, and don't want to give anything up. But I'm constantly tired, I often crib my sermons off the Internet, and I'm not much fun at home. I don't how much longer I can keep this up."

Craig and Susan represent countless ministers who are desperately trying to be faithful and effective pastors but whose many ministerial demands are pushing them to their spiritual, physical, professional, and relational limits. They work at least fifty hours each week and then sleeplessly reflect about their ministry late at night or early in the morning for another twenty more. A recent survey of Lutheran Church–Missouri Synod pastors noted that although 30 percent found ministry fulfilling and 30 percent saw their ministerial life as moderately satisfying; nevertheless, 40 percent of Missouri Synod pastors described themselves as moderately depressed and bounding on professional burnout.[2] Could it be that nearly half the pastoral work force is dissatisfied with their lives and ministries? These figures represent a growing professional and spiritual malaise in ministry across denominational lines—many of today's best pastors are burning out, not shining forth the light of God with great spiritual energy and creativity!

While many factors contribute to feelings of burnout and brownout among today's ministers, we believe that loss of pastoral vitality is intimately related to the many small but cumulatively significant choices pastors make every day, most of which reveal a pervasive neglect of daily practices of self-care, spiritual and relational well-being, and continuing theological and professional nurture. Seminaries, pastors, and congregations are all responsible, in part, for this neglect.

Our goal in this book is to enable pastors to claim their power and shine forth as Christian leaders with fiery and creative energy through focusing on very specific practices through which they can experience renewed vitality, improved health, and spiritual growth for facing the complex challenges of doing ministry in the twenty-first century. While we recognize that all ministry is contextual and take seriously the insights of family systems theory—psychologically informed insights about pathology and codependence—and the ongoing quests of feminist/womanist and liberation theology to inform the context of ministry and congregational life, our primary focus here will be on life-transforming spiritual and professional practices that will enable pastors to live out their vocations over a lifetime with wisdom, effectiveness, energy, health, and compassion. As pastors, we are called to "feed the fire" of pastoral vitality and excellence by opening to God's lively energy through a variety of ancient and contemporary practices that promote wholeness and spiritual transformation. The gospel of John proclaims that Jesus came that we might have life and have it abundantly (John 10:10)! We believe that Jesus' mission to bring abundant life to humankind applies to pastors, too!

As a clergy couple who have been committed to joining vital and healthy ministry in both our personal and professional lives for almost three decades, we have observed many times over that hard fact that the health of a congregation is intimately related to the health of its pastoral leader or leaders. Right now, we believe that what our churches need, more than anything else, are healthy, innovative, and spiritually energized pastors.

We are delighted that Lancaster Theological Seminary, with support of the Lilly Endowment, has established three pastoral excellence and well-being programs that address this concern: a Wholeness in Ministry program for pastors in their first congregational call, following graduation from seminary; a Renewing Ministry program for experienced pastors in mid-career; and a Harvesting Wisdom program for pastors preparing for retirement. Bruce has had the opportunity to be the director and primary architect of these ministerial transformation programs. In addition, as coleaders of several of these groups, both Bruce and Kate have been able to observe first-hand the challenges of contemporary ministry as well as the practices and attitudes that support ministerial health and vitality. Kate's observations are also informed by her work as a pastoral counselor, denominational mentor, and spiritual director with both seminarians and pastors.

Based on our experience we believe strongly that, in the interplay of God's call and our response as pastors, pastors who are truly committed to living God's vision, shalom and wholeness can rekindle, sustain, and enliven God's fire in their lives and in the lives of those with whom they pastor! We invite you to join us on this journey of "becoming fire" in ministry.

BURNOUT OR TRANSFORMATION?

Mark's Gospel provides us with an insightful glimpse into the challenges of ministry in the first century as well as our own time. After training his disciples in the arts of ministry, Jesus sends them into the world on their own to heal the sick, cast out demons, and preach the good news of God's coming reign. The disciples excitedly report back to Jesus with news of their ministerial successes (Mark 6:7–13, 30). Wisely recognizing that the disciples need time for rest, recreation, and prayer, Jesus counsels them to "come away to a deserted place all by yourselves and rest awhile." The passage continues, "For many were coming and going, and they had no leisure even to eat," and so they went away in the boat to a deserted place by themselves for rest, prayer, and renewal (Mark 6:31–32).

A few chapters earlier, Mark describes Jesus practicing what he counsels in terms of his own prayer life. We are told that, after a day filled with teaching, healing, and social activities, "in the morning, while it was still dark, he got up and went to a deserted place, and there he prayed" (Mark 1:35). But, quite realistically, neither contemplative retreat story ends with an undisturbed season of prayerful rest being gained for either the teacher or his disciples. Sadly, effective and insightful ministry creates greater demands on the pastor's time and makes it all the more difficult for the pastor to get away for rest and reflection. Mark notes that while Jesus was praying, "Simon and his companions hunted for him. When they found him, they said to him, 'Everyone is looking for you.'" Does this sound familiar? Is it your experience that the minute you close the door to pray or meditate, prepare for a contemplative walk, reflect on the lectionary texts, or pick up a long-neglected theological text, the phone always seems to ring or you hear a knock on the study door, or the secretary comes to you with an urgent request? Like Jesus and his first followers, we must decide in that moment how best to respond to persons who believe that they are in need of our immediate spiritual counsel, practical advice, or healing presence. As we seek to draw boundaries, the challenge is to be gentle and compassionate with both ourselves and others as we balance love of self with love of other.

Mark 6 describes Jesus' response to the interruptions to ministry in terms of the interplay of contemplation and compassion. When he saw that the crowds had followed him to the other side of the lake and were waiting for him to disembark, Jesus "had compassion on them, because they were like sheep without a shepherd" (Mark 6:34). Knowing that interruption is inevitable in ministry, could it be that Jesus intentionally and proactively made time for prayer and meditation so that he could respond with compassion, and not irritation, to the demands of persons in need? Could it be that just a few well chosen minutes of solitude enabled him to return to his ministerial tasks, refreshed and revitalized, and able to discern clearly those particular persons to whom he was called to mediate God's healing touch?

While it is impossible to entirely manage your time in Christian ministry, Jesus' approach to ministry reminds us that we *can* learn to be intentional in our own practice of ministry. Take a moment, now, to recall the most recent unexpected interruption in your quiet time of reflection, study, or prayer. What was the nature of the interruption? When did it occur? In what ways did it alter your schedule? How did you feel at the time? Was the interruption one that could have been avoided? How else might you have handled the interruption?

Ideally, when we are in tune with God's lively energy in our lives, we believe that ministerial interruptions can call us to prayerful hospitality and welcome. Interruptions can become synchronous moments through which God calls us to be partners in compassion and transformation for both ourselves and others. But we must be prepared, through our spiritual practices and self-care, to have a heart of compassion when unexpected interruptions arise in our tightly scheduled days.

Authentic pastoral crises can occur at any hour of the day, and we recognize that pastors must often choose to drop everything, including holiday plans or time with their own families, in order to visit a family in shock over the sudden death of a loved one, a congregant who has been rushed to the emergency room, or a youth whose depression has led to a suicide attempt. In such moments, the call for pastoral presence is clear and unmistakable. However, healthy and vital ministry over the long haul is a product of cumulative, daily decision-making that balances ministerial creativity and availability with care for the pastor's own personal and relational wholeness, amidst a wide array of pastoral care situations in which much spiritual and personal discernment is required.

Mark's description of a "day in the life of Jesus" (Mark 1:21–39) presents Jesus as a model of creative decision making and self-differentiation. When Peter and the disciples urge Jesus to settle permanently in Capernaum in a classic example of ministerial triangulation, he doesn't argue with them but clearly states that his highest priority is to preach the gospel in neighboring towns. Jesus finds his spiritual center in the silence from which all discernment of divine direction emerges.

For many years, Bruce taught at Georgetown University School of Medicine. In the course of his first year seminar on spirituality and medicine, he routinely asked his medical students, "In what ways do you need to shape your life in order to be glad twenty years from now that you entered the field of medicine?" Well aware of the high incidence of substance abuse, mental illness, and divorce among physicians, Bruce wanted to remind his students that a well-lived professional life was a matter of personal choice as well as good fortune. Today, Bruce challenges seminary students and newly ordained pastors with the same question, "Twenty years from now, will you be thankful that you entered the ministry? Just as importantly, will your children and spouse or partner be equally grateful for your commitment to ministry?"

Whether secular or religious, the life of a professional caregiver is difficult in today's multitasking, globally connected, postmodern era. Ministers and other caregivers can learn much from Sandra Bloom's insights about our society's high level of trauma and trauma victimization. In her book *Creating Sanctuary: Toward the Evolution of Sane Societies*, Bloom suggests that there is a need for creating trauma-sensitive sanctuaries in churches, schools, and other service delivery organizations, which can give respite not only for our society's many trauma victims but also for those front-line caregivers (such as pastors, doctors, nurses, social workers, and teachers) who receive "secondary traumatization" simply through caregiving for trauma victims in systems that retraumatize them. Bloom's work affirms the importance of faithful and disciplined pastors who intentionally take time to create sanctuaries for healing for *themselves* as well as for their congregants, communities, and families away from the violent barrage of needs "coming at you fast" in our trauma-laden world.[3]

Moving into a more positive mode, we believe that just as ministerial burnout is partly a matter of choice, so too, are opportunities for ministerial transformation. Today's pastors do not have to repeat the mistakes of their predecessors in ministry even though congregants often goad them into doing so. Instead, they can mindfully follow Paul's admonition in terms of their own vocation to "be not conformed to this world, but be transformed by the renewing of your mind" (Rom. 12:2). Pastors *can* commit themselves to choosing healing and wholeness, rather than addictive patterns of organizational "success."[4]

Reclaiming vital, healthy, and effective ministry amidst the competing expectations of others is not easy. Feeding the fire of pastoral transformation over the long haul calls us to be intentional about *creating sanctuaries* for our own physical and emotional health, intimate relationships, and spiritual formation. We must not succumb to popular patterns of professional success foisted upon us by our congregants and social norms. Far too often these models of "successful" ministry actually mask a pastor's compulsive and addictive behaviors, excessive need for approval, and the unseen cost of emotional neglect and growing alienation within his or her family.

At such moments of decision making, we are reminded of the question that Jesus asked the man by the side of the pool at Bethesda who had suffered from paralysis for thirty-eight years, "Do you want to be made well?" Although the man gave Jesus legitimate reasons for his lifelong paralysis, Jesus invited him into a creative partnership in creating an alternative future with the words, "Stand up, take your mat and walk" (John 5:1–9).

Today, consider Jesus asking you a similar question. Do you want to be a healthy and vital pastor? Do you want to experience joy in ministry? Do you want your ministry to be a blessing to your family as well as your congregation? Do you want to feed the fire of life-transforming ministry?

Although you can always give reasons for your choices to conform to dysfunctional, self-sacrificing models of ministry given you by many of your predecessors, by God's grace God will continue to ask if you truly want to be a healthy and vital pastor. God will patiently listen to the same old excuses that will allow you to continue your harmful behavior patterns, but God also continually invites you to take the first steps toward ministerial wholeness in your life. Instead of asking you to "Stand up, take your mat and walk," God, we believe, challenges you to "become changed into fire!"

Take a few minutes and go back over the stories of Craig and Susan, the two pastors with which this chapter began. Is their experience similar to yours? Reflect on where you are in your ministry today: How do you feel about your ministry? What practices, if any, help you stay vital and alive in ministry? Are you "browning out," "burning out," or "shining forth" with spiritual enthusiasm, physical and emotional energy, and vigor in ministry? Can you imagine practicing ministry in a more healthy and effective way than you are currently doing? Do you want to make changes in your ministry so that you can be more spiritually centered, attentive and loving to friends and family, and effective and compassionate toward your parishioners? If your answer is "yes" to the final question, you have already taken the first step on the road to pastoral transformation! You can become fire, shining forth the light and warmth of God's love in a ministry that can truly transform not only your congregation but the world!

Tom is a pastor who chose to feed the fire of ministerial excellence and well-being. By his own admission, he did everything right in terms of his denomination's pastoral expectations after he was called to pastor a congregation in a growing California suburb. He followed all the principles of church growth and new member assimilation. He worked tirelessly to reach out to the neighborhood and gather a group of spiritual leaders within his growing congregation. He was on fire for God, and his congregation grew by leaps and bounds. The small multipurpose room, initially utilized as sanctuary and social hall, mushroomed into a large "campus" with a state of the art worship center and Christian education wing. Although he had been faithful and could still produce an inspiring sermon at the drop of a hat, Tom began to notice that he was losing his spiritual and pastoral fire. "I was the envy of many of my peers. My church was lifted up in the denomination as a success story. But, over time, I noticed that although I could excite my congregation from the pulpit, my sermons seemed superficial to me. I also noticed that my prayer life was flat. I spoke glowingly about our growing youth program and outreach in the community, but seldom saw my own kids at church or at home." One day, Tom realized that if he didn't change his approach to ministry, he would soon burn out and lose the holy fire that had inspired him in the beginning. "I experienced a conversion—twenty years after I first accepted Christ as my savior. I knew I had to die to my old image of ministry to be reborn to a new image of ministry that honored God *and* my family."

Tom asked for, and received, a sabbatical six months earlier than the church had initially planned. He took extra time with his children and went on a second honeymoon with his wife. He found a holistic spiritual director, who combined spiritual direction with a concern for physical well-being. Tom began to practice centering prayer and took time out each week for spiritual retreat. Today he says, "My life has been transformed, and so has my ministry. God is alive again for me. I've found my calling again, to be a teacher and spiritual guide. I'm working less, delegating more, and, believe it or not, our church is still growing." Tom chose to "feed the fire" of ministry, and the light of God still shines brightly in his ministry because of it.

LIGHT ON THE PATH

In one of the great "I am" sayings from John's Gospel, Jesus proclaims, "I am the light of the world. Whoever follows me will never walk in darkness but will have the light of life" (John 8:12). John's Gospel proclaims that God's light is the "light of all people" (John 1:4) and that God's true light "enlightens everyone" (John 1:9). Although the reality of spiritual darkness abounds in the world, it can never overcome God's creative and transforming light. Matthew's gospel records an even bolder claim for Jesus' followers:

> You are the light of the world. A city built on a hill cannot be hid. No one after lighting a lamp puts it under the bushel basket, but on the lampstand, and it gives light to all in the house. In the same way, let your light shine before others, so that they may see your good works and give glory to your [Parent] in heaven. (Matt. 5:14–16)

We wonder what it would look like for today's harried pastors faced with brownout and burnout to embrace fully Jesus' promise, "you are the light of the world. Yes, you are God's fire in the world." While God's light shines in all persons, today's pastors have a unique vocation as God's light bearers. As pastors, we are the children of the shaman, prophets, and healers of ancient times. Aware that we have been touched by God in a personal way, we are called to share our experiences of God with others so that they might also claim the "light of life" as their own deepest reality.

Like Isaiah in the Temple, most pastors have experienced, dramatically or subtly, a spiritual encounter that changed their lives. Whether gradual or unexpected, a holy presence larger than our own speaks within our lives, asking "whom shall I send, and who shall go for us?" and we respond, like Isaiah, with fear and trembling, "Here am I: send me!" (Isa. 6:1–8)

What do you remember about your experience of God's call to ministry? According to family legend, Bruce's father Everett, who served as an American Baptist pastor in congregations and substance abuse programs for more than thirty years, never had an earth-shaking experience of call, yet he preached to chickens as a small boy, growing up on the family farm. Though he wasn't ordained until he was in his late thirties, Bruce's father experienced God's subtle lure toward preaching and pastoral care as early as seven years old.

Suzanne, who spent many years as an oncology nurse before going to seminary, experienced the call to ministry during a women's spirituality retreat at Kirkridge Retreat and Conference Center in Pennsylvania. While she was walking the labyrinth, she heard a voice speak to her, "You are my beloved daughter. You are a healer. But now I want you to heal spirits as well as bodies." Following her call experience, Suzanne sought out a spiritual guide who was open to mystical experiences. After many weeks of conversation and prayer, Suzanne chose to enroll in seminary and is now a United Church of Christ pastor.

Bruce sees his call as subtle and lifelong. From a rather emotional born-again experience at the "Round Up for God" revival meeting at age nine, through a lively adolescent adventure into the world of psychedelics, meditation, and Asian religions in the late 1960s and early '70s, and then a rediscovery of progressive Christianity in graduate school, Bruce felt a holy calling toward ministry in higher education. But midway through his graduate studies at Claremont Graduate University, a gentle movement within his spirit invited him to join the pulpit and the classroom. As Bruce notes, "Nothing dramatic happened. But over time I came to realize that my vocation was to share the gospel of a positive and life-transforming Christianity that joined the intellect and the emotions, theology and practice, and liberal theology with evangelical and mystical experience. As I pondered this gentle call in graduate school, I realized that God had been quietly working in the conservative faith of my childhood Baptist church, the ecstatic experiences of the 'summer of love,' the centering moments of transcendental and Christian meditation, and the insights of process theology. My relationship to Kate was the tipping point. I respected her gifts and knew that together we could make a difference in lives on campus and in congregations." For nearly thirty years, Bruce has joined pulpit and classroom as a university chaplain, seminary professor, author and lecturer, interim pastor, and, currently, as pastor of a progressive congregation.

Kate dedicated herself to serving God at age thirteen around the campfire at Camp Christian, a Disciples of Christ conference center in Ohio. Years later, as a student at Scripps College in Claremont, California, Kate had a mystical experience in which she saw fiery letters etched on a grey stone. According to Kate, "I knew that my life work would involve finding out the meaning of these mysterious and fiery words." Anticipating a career in the field of teaching religion, a few years later when she was program director for the Stanford University YWCA, Kate discovered that the path opened for her to become an ordained minister after she encountered two dynamic feminist clergywomen in campus ministry, Diane Kenney and Barbara Troxell. Having encountered sexually exploitative male ministers during the formative years of her career development in the '60s and '70s, Kate has doggedly pursued her call to nurturing God's shalom, healing and wholeness, for herself and others. Her belief in God's ever present guidance speaking through dreams and synchronous relational encounters has kept her spirit "aglow" for the past thirty years in various part- and full-time congregational, campus, pastoral counseling, and spiritual direction ministries, which she has always sought to balance with her duties as a parent and as a caregiver for her mother, who has lived with us for a number of years.

Virtually every pastor can identify moments when he or she experienced God's presence and call as vibrant and life-transforming. Not something to be seen as "Pollyanna" or naively superficial, rather these transformative moments have often followed a time of deep suffering, alienation, or loss and represent an experience of great spiritual and emotional healing. Like the shaman and prophet of old, a pastor's initial experiences of "deep calling to deep," partaking of God's "holy adventure," change everything. For a moment, the whole earth is "full of God's glory" (Isa. 6:3) as her or his own life experience becomes what Celtic Christians call a "thin place," a transparent reality in which the light of the divine shines brightly through, uniting the sacred and the secular, the divine and human. In moments of call, these future pastors speak of seeing themselves and God in a new, brightly shining light as their horizon of experience shifted from the everyday to that which is sacred and eternal.

For pastors who have experienced such moments of "enlightenment," either by synchronicity or the rigors of a regular commitment to spiritual practices, Marcus Borg's description of Jesus as a "spirit person" makes a lot of sense. Indeed, we believe that we pastors, like Jesus, are all called to be "spirit persons" in our time. A "spirit person" is one who not only has "vivid and frequent experiences of another world or dimension of reality," but who can also reveal these dimensions or realities to others. As a spirit person, Jesus was "a conduit for the power or wisdom of God to enter the world."[5] When Jesus promised his disciples that they could do "greater works" in their ministries than he had accomplished (John 14:12), he was challenging his followers to become spirit persons like himself—teachers, mystics, healers, and prophets—whose intimacy with God would enable them to become God's partners in healing persons, institutions, and the world. Jesus was inviting his first followers—and is still inviting today's pastors—to become spirit persons, whose lives become lights of the world, guiding, energizing, and transforming others as a byproduct of their own grounded and centered spiritual energy.

Today we pastors still wear the mantle of prophet, shaman, and healer whether or not we recognize and claim it. One day at a youth group retreat, a teenager broke her toe. While she and Kate waited for her mother to come and take her to the emergency room to have the toe X-rayed, Kate gently enfolded the girl's toe with her hands to bring comfort and warmth. When the girl later exclaimed to her mother, "Kate is a good pastor, mom, because she took away the pain in my toe," Kate began to realize that she was more "aglow" with the spirit than she had previously imagined!

Most of us entered ministry in order to experience and share God's lively and world-transforming spirit, and yet we are mere infants when it comes to understanding the spiritual power we hold in our hands! Most of us experienced God's transforming, healing love at the heart of our lives at some point and desperately wanted to share that experience with others in our ministries. Sadly, however, many of us have had to look beyond our denominations and seminaries to find the kind of resources that would nurture and deepen this initial spiritual glow in a way that allows us to remain faithful mediators of God's spirit to our congregants, churches, communities, and the world.

Where in our lives are we called to begin our pursuit of daily rekindling the fire of God's inspiration and movement? In addition to committing ourselves to daily practices of creative spiritual formation, we must also open ourselves regularly to imaginative and creative theological reflection and education.

TRANSFORMING THEOLOGY

The foundations of a growing and glowing healthy ministry must be both spiritual and theological. These theological foundations must be holistic—joining body, mind, and spirit with social dynamics in a web of mutually supportive relationships. We believe that the most creative holistic theology joins vision, promise, and practice. *Vision* in ministry involves the interplay of a pastor's theological worldview and the concreteness of her or his personal and professional life. *Promise* involves God's assurance that we can experience our theological vision in everyday life. Put in the language of the Sermon on the Mount, our vocation is to be "lights of the world," and this can only be embodied by "letting our light shine" in compassionate acts of service to the world. *Practice* involves our commitment to regular spiritual disciplines and actions that not only reflect our theological assumptions but creatively embrace the whole of our professional, personal, and relational lives. As Craig Dykstra notes, "practices are those cooperative human activities through which we, as individuals and communities, grow and develop in moral character and substance."[6] Holistic theology supports our ministerial call through promoting practices that enable us to experience and sustain God's spiritual fire in our ministries as we ever more fully incarnate God's transforming and healing light throughout our lives. This call to become lively spirit persons like Jesus challenges pastors to continue to evolve and grow in wisdom and stature as we increasingly incarnate and share God's healing light through ministries of vision, promise, and practice.

We have discovered that a healthy ministerial *vision* is best grounded in the affirmation that God is present and inspires every moment and season of life and ministry. The call to ministry challenges us to be able to name and claim God's call in each moment of our lives, no matter how difficult or painful that moment might be. If, as the Apostle Paul asserts, God is the one "in whom we live, move, and have our being" (Acts 17:28), then our prayers of intercession are best followed, as our own congregation prays, with the affirmation that "God is in all things. All things are in God!" The doctrine of divine omnipresence invites us to see all events in our lives and ministries as divinely inspired and affirms that God's call abounds in both the spiritual and secular, Christian and non-Christian, spheres of life. With Brother Lawrence, we can assert that our particular call to ministry is part of a much larger divine call within our lives and the world.[7]

Like Sophia, or Divine Wisdom, described in Proverbs 8, God calls us at the street corners and in the marketplace as well as in the still, small voice within our spirits. God addresses each of us intimately and personally in our time and place. Along with one of our theology professors, John Cobb, we affirm that God calls pastors "forward" toward the creative transformation of their ministries so that they might be God's partners in the healing and enlivening of their families, congregations, and the world.

So it is that when the Prologue of the Gospel of John affirms that God's light *enlightens everyone*, we can personally affirm the truth that "God is enlightening me even when I am unaware of it." We can expect to be transformed in ministry, as in all things, because God is always doing a new thing in the world and in our lives. This is surely good news for browned out pastors who want to shine forth in holy fire and burned out pastors who pray desperately for spiritual resurrection. God continually gives us visions of transformed and healthy selves through the inspiration of scripture, insights gained through reflective moments with a spiritual director or colleague group, and various ministries of healing and wholeness such as pastoral counseling, centering prayer or reiki, as well as through the quiet whispers of wisdom that come to us in dreams and sighs too deep for words. Deep down, God says to each of us, over and over again, "If any pastor is in Christ, he is a new creation; if any pastor is in Christ, she is a new creation!"

So God's call toward healthy and vital ministry is both personal and interpersonal. It is multifaceted in nature. It is enriched by our commitment to daily disciplines of body, mind, and spirit and by our willingness to open ourselves and our imaginations to creative new theological horizons. If we notice, pause, open, yield, and respond to God's gentle lures towards healing and wholeness, we can hear God calling us moment by moment, whether it is preaching preparation or congregational visioning, planning vacations with our spouse or partner, lacing up our shoes for a prayer-power walk, or gazing into the face of a our child or a good friend.

Like Annie Dillard's "tree with lights in it," we can be suddenly awakened in the midst of our lives by the gentle glow of divine guidance and inspiration that has been there all along, just waiting for us to notice. Like Jacob, we can awaken from a dream to discover that our ordinary lives are filled with angelic encounters, and exclaim, "God was in this place—and now I know it" (Gen. 28:10–17, paraphrase).

In conclusion, we challenge you to remember the *promise* of God's vision—that you *can* become fire in ministry. You can *be* what you *see*. You *can* embody God's abundant life and out of that abundance, you *can* give life and light to others. You *can* become God's partner in transforming your congregation. Like the woman with the hemorrhage, you *can* experience divine power flowing through you to transform your life and energize your ministry. As a conduit of Christ's lively spiritual energy, you *can* let God's light flow in and through you to the world: your family, friends, congregation, and community.

Yet, the promise is worth little without practice! This book is dedicated to enabling you to *practice* lively, energetic, healthy, and visionary ministry at every stage of your ministerial journey. Because each pastor's spiritual journey is unique, our goal is to present spiritual and professional pathways that you can practice according to your age, pastoral context, personality type, and relational situation. As Tony Robinson notes, leadership is always "a spiritual practice."[8] We seek to present a way of life that will enable you to discern God's lively and visionary presence in terms of your physical well-being, ongoing theological education, spiritual formation, relationships, attitude toward time, administrative leadership, and unique personality and gifts. We embrace Christian ministry as a "holy adventure" that encompasses the whole person—body, mind, and spirit—and all his or her relationships. We believe that your unique holy adventure in ministry and personal life is part of a larger Holy Adventure that is God's own exciting and holy quest to transform and heal the church and all creation. We have been called to ministry for just "such a time as this," in which our own commitment to wholeness will enable us and our congregations to be healthy and creative partners in healing the world.

FEEDING THE MINISTERIAL FIRE

A note or two about the methodology employed in this book. Because we are committed to a practical theology that joins vision, promise, and practice, each chapter concludes with suggestions for spiritual practices that will nurture wholeness and vitality in your life. Dorothy Bass notes, "Practices are those shared activities that address fundamental human needs and that, woven together, form a way of life."[9] In the context of the many challenges of ministry today, we believe that a lively commitment to holistic spiritual practices enables pastors to sustain their call to ministry, awakens their creative energy for visionary congregational leadership, and enables them to experience God's healing and enlightening fire in their lives. These spiritual practices feed our ministerial fire and enable us to be aflame with creativity and love even in challenging situations.

In specific, each chapter will conclude with suggestions for integrating traditional and innovative spiritual practices, undertaking specific healthy ministerial behaviors, using spiritual affirmations, and establishing a covenant with God for your wholeness and vitality. We assume that you will modify any practice to suit your own spiritual needs, experiences, or personality type. Our goal is to present a wide variety of spiritual possibilities for ministerial transformation at every season of life and congregational context.

A Holistic Spiritual Formation Exercise

Take a few moments to meditate upon Thomas Merton's story of two North African Desert Fathers. Listening to your own life, what is your current spiritual temperature? Where do you need to "become changed into fire"?

How would becoming fire, or glowingly embodying God's healing and transforming light, change your life and ministry?

Take some time simply to breathe gently but deeply. Let your rhythmic, slow breathing calm your mind, body, and spirit. If your attention shifts or you find yourself distracted by thoughts, simply bring your attention back to your breath without any negative judgment.

Now we invite you to visualize a divine, healing light, entering your whole being with every breath. With each breath, experience this divine light gently filling your mind, your sinuses, relieving any tension or fatigue. Visualize it filling your head and moving on down through your neck, shoulders, and spinal column, gradually filling your chest and abdomen, cleansing, relaxing, and renewing you as it flows downward, all the way through your pelvis and thighs, knees, calves, and ankles, all the way down to the soles of your feet. Visualize yourself glowing radiantly as a "light of the world" in every cell of your body. See yourself moving through your day as a brightly shining being of light. Now, bringing your focus back into the present moment, we invite you to make a commitment to live by the light, bringing light to every personal and pastoral encounter now and throughout the upcoming week. Close with a brief prayer of gratitude for the light that shines in all things and shines brightly through you, renewing and energizing you for ministry.

A Practice for Healthy Ministry

Brother Lawrence invited his companions to practice the presence of God in the everyday acts of monastic life, whether working in the kitchen, buying provisions, greeting strangers, or sharing in worship. Ministry is made up of countless ordinary acts, practiced over and over again. While the many acts of ministry can fragment our lives, they can also form a seamlessly woven way of life.

One way to experience the unity of divine presence is to "breathe" your ministry. One of our spiritual teachers, Allan Armstrong Hunter, counseled us to "breathe the spirit of God deeply in and give it gratefully back again." With the psalmist who proclaims, "let everything that breathes praise God" (Psa. 150:6), we suggest that each breath can become a prayer. The tradition of breath prayer has its roots in eastern meditation. So it is that Vietnamese Buddhist spirit teacher Thich Nhat Hanh counsels that conscious awareness of our breath is essential to spiritual growth, especially in challenging situations. This insightful spiritual teacher, who often dialogues with Christians, suggests the following breathing exercise:

> *Breathing in, I calm my body.*
> *Breathing out, I smile.*
> *Dwelling in the present moment,*
> *I know this is a wonderful moment!*[10]

Throughout the week, notice your breath. When are you breathless? When is your breath calm and peaceful? When do you experience your breath as shallow and anxious? What is it like for you to take a few moments to gently slow and deepen your breath? Can you combine this awareness with a conscious intention to breathe in God's spirit with each breath and give it gently back again with an attitude of gratitude?

We invite you to make a commitment to breathe consciously through your more difficult pastoral tasks. You might choose to begin by breathing consciously through your easier tasks as well! For example, when the phone rings, take a moment to breathe in God's spirit before answering. When you check your e-mail, take a few breaths of opening to God's centering spirit while your Internet desktop comes up. When you come to the church office, rather than immediately beginning to work, take a few minutes to breathe calmly and gently as you walk from your car to the office, or when you first arrive at your study's desk. When someone knocks on the door, take a moment to breathe in God's spirit as you greet your visitor. At congregational meetings, when you experience your anxiety rising, rather than tapping your foot or entering into a defensive conversation, consider breathing in God's spirit in whom we "live and move and have our being." Notice your body relaxing as you center in a quiet place where you are free to think creatively and not defensively. When you come home from work, take a moment to breathe in God's presence as you enter your home. With your breath, bless your home and any who dwell there with you.

An Affirmation of Faith

Faith is grounded in our vision of reality. Historic and contemporary confessions and affirmations of faith are, at their best, guideposts pointing toward a certain ineffable vision of reality. For example, to affirm that "God is the maker of heaven and earth" is to proclaim that the whole of the earth and the whole of our lives all reveal divine wisdom and guidance and that every moment can be and *is* a holy and inspirational moment.

When we live daily with repeated (spoken or written) faith affirmations that are authentic to the best of our faith experiences, we begin to experience the world more fully in terms of these deeply held beliefs.[11] Over time, our character and way of life come to reflect these most deeply held theological and personal affirmations. If you can authentically embrace any of the following life-transforming affirmations, we invite you to embrace their truth more deeply by repeating them over and over again throughout the week.

- God's healing light shines in my life and ministry.
- By God's grace, I am the light of the world, giving light to others.
- I embody God's abundant life and healing presence in every aspect of my life and ministry.

Feel free to write your affirmations on note paper that you can easily post on your computer, bathroom mirror, or dashboard of your car. Make a special effort to notice when you begin to feel anxious or fall back into unhealthy patterns of ministry and take a minute or two to pause and recite them to yourself, opening and yielding the situation to God.

A Covenant of Wholeness and Vitality in Ministry

Healthy, vital, and effective ministry is a matter of choice as well as grace. We can choose to take the first steps in becoming lively, nonanxious and transforming pastoral leaders by consciously choosing to open ourselves to God's "fire"—the energy of God's light and life. Indeed, life is an ongoing call and response in which God calls us repeatedly within each moment to choose light and life. By our conscious openness to God in each moment, we say "yes" to God's transformation of our lives and ministry.

In your own words or in the words provided below, we invite you to respond to Jesus' question, "Do you want to be made well?" We invite you to make a covenant to say:

"Yes! I want to be a healthy and vital pastor. I covenant to walk God's path of shalom—healing and wholeness in mind, body, spirit, and relationships."

Remember this covenant as you choose your personal and ministerial path throughout the week.

T W O

GLORIFYING GOD IN YOUR BODY

Embodiment is at the heart of Jewish and Christian theology. How we treat our bodies ultimately reflects our theology of incarnation, embodiment, and divine presence. The biblical vision of creation describes the universe as a lively reflection of the joyfully dancing Wisdom of God (Prov. 8). The world in all its complexity and wonder is described in the liturgy of Genesis 1 as "good" in its rhythm of rest and action, human and nonhuman, earth and heaven.

The New Testament proclaims that salvation comes through incarnation: "the word was made flesh and lived among us, and we have seen [the Word's] glory" (John 1:14). God's creative word is the source and inspiration of the whole creation—including the human mind, body, and spirit (John 1:1–5, 9). God "enlightens" all creation from the cells of our bodies to the sun and stars in the sky. So it is that the New Testament vision of resurrection—for Jesus and for all of us—proclaims that salvation is to be found in embodied existence. The resurrection of Jesus, as understood by Paul in

1 Corinthians 15 and in the Gospel narratives, suggests that our hope beyond the grave is to be found in the transformation of the whole person, including the transformation and healing of our physical embodiment, as well as in the fulfillment of our spiritual lives and relationships.

Jesus' healing ministry reveals God's all-inclusive affirmation of embodiment as a vehicle of salvation. As a sign of the coming reign of God's shalom—peace, healing, and wholeness for all the world—Jesus healed the sick, touching bodies with his hands, speaking words of forgiveness, exorcism, and challenge, and using first-century medical remedies such as mud and saliva. Among the great spiritual figures of humankind, Jesus is unique in his affirmation of the tightly woven interrelationship between the healing of body, mind, and spirit. The Gospel authors portray Jesus as a truly holistic healer who, when he touches the sick, not only liberates them from the shackles of their physical illness, but also transforms their spiritual lives, future life possibilities, and place in the social and religious order. Jesus' healing ministry demonstrates God's broadly inclusive desire for healing and wholeness for persons in every dimension of their lives: political, emotional, spiritual, socioeconomic, as well as physical.[1]

Jesus' witness to the reality of divine omnipresence reveals not only that the heavens declare the glory of God, but that divine harmony, beauty, and wisdom are present even in the intricate workings of our immune, digestive, and cardiovascular systems as well as in our spiritual practices and in techniques of Western and complementary medical practices. The practical meaning of divine omnipresence is the basic affirmation that God is the ever-present multidimensional "lure" toward harmony and beauty, truth and goodness that orders and animates all things, including our bodies. If the primary vehicle of vital ministry is the holistic integrity (body, mind, and spirit) of the pastor, as we suggest, then a lifelong pursuit of "lively embodiment" of God's vision of abundant life is essential to ministerial vitality and effectiveness.

In this context, consider for a moment the Apostle Paul's affirmation that "your body is the temple of the Holy Spirit within you, which you have from God" (1 Cor. 6:19). What does it mean for you to truly honor your body as "temple of the Holy Spirit?" How does it transform the way you experience your body and make time for its daily care? In light of Paul's image of the body as the "temple of the Holy Spirit," what would it look like for you to "tithe"—to dedicate at least 10 percent of your waking hours—to caring for your body? For someone who rises at 7 AM and goes to bed at 11 PM that would mean approximately one and a half hours a day dedicated to some form of self-care, such as meditation, physical exercise, and prayer, which holistically integrates care for one's body, mind, and spirit.

If you are created in God's image and you affirm that your uniquely embodied personhood reflects God's desire for wholeness and beauty, then what can you do to affirm God's grace and beauty reflected in your particular body type and physical condition? Even if you face a challenging chronic or life-threatening illness, how can you mediate God's spirit in and through it in your ministry?

Despite compelling evidence that we as Christian ministers are called to live out of a holistic vision of divine omnipresence and embodied incarnation, we are saddened to find that so many pastors are apparently "practical Gnostics." Although they do not deny the existence of the physical body or the goodness of divine embodiment, their lack of significant daily commitments of time and energy for self-care suggests that their bodies have little or no role in their ministries or spiritual lives. We believe that our ministries are undermined and our sense of vocation diminished when we neglect to care for our own bodies. As our bodies burn out, our ministerial hopes and visions often go with them!

Kate, who has always worked hard at self-care, believed that she had truly failed at this effort when, during the year of her church's eightieth anniversary celebration, she found herself having to get a heart pacemaker. She thought back on the fact that she had consciously decided to "give her all" to make that year a landmark year in the life of her congregation, but she had always tried to pace herself. It was several years later that she discovered that the cause of her heart irregularity was arsenic poisoning due to her extended labors sanding and cleaning a very large two-story deck made of arsenic laden pressure treated lumber. At the time the pacemaker was put in, neither her cardiologist nor Kate had connected the two circumstances. Kate's confidence in her ability to pace herself and exercise responsible self-care was renewed after she followed a simple detoxification diet for ten days and a variety of physical and neurological symptoms (including heartbeat irregularity) all went away and have never come back! Kate jokes that even being the most highly informed and dedicated practitioner of self-care does not substitute for ignorance about avoiding basic environmental hazards!

Mary is a pastor who believes that she can never do enough for God. She works from sunrise to sunset, rushing from meeting to meeting, barely taking time to eat. After a quick supper with her family, she heads back to church most evenings for meetings that typically last until 10:00 P.M. Mary's practice of ministry reflects her overinflated sense of indispensability to God and her church. "There's just so much to do, and our congregation is poised to become a real factor in the religious life of our city. I don't want to let my people down, and I don't want to let God down either. I just can't do enough, and if I quit, God will be disappointed in me. The only way I can take some time off right now is to get sick." Mary sees her body as a machine and she expects to use until it wears out from unceasing wear and tear. She has recently been diagnosed with an autoimmune disease triggered by stress.

Mike is following a similarly unhealthy path in ministry as is Mary, but, as Kate's mother would say, "He is cruising for a bruising!" Mike says, "When God called me to ministry in midlife, I knew I had to place God's call above everything else, including my family. This hasn't been easy, but God calls us to sacrifice. The world needs socially conscious congregations and pastors. That's my calling, and if it means long nights at the city council or homeless shelter, so be it. Seventy hours is not enough to offer God, but I give what I can." Although he routinely works seventy hours a week, Mike jokes somewhat ironically that he is an example of "better living through chemistry," as he takes numerous medications for high cholesterol, hypertension, and stress. Although they are often cited by colleagues and denominational leaders as successful models of ministry, Mary and Mike have been unfaithful to God in their care for themselves and their families.

Our concern for all the Marys and Mikes in ministry goes beyond issues of physical and relational health. We question the soundness of the theological vision that motivates their frenetic action and we worry about their preaching and teaching this unhealthy theology to their congregants. To be sure, their codependent concept of ministry probably reflects their relationships in their family of origin, but its unexamined practice not only disempowers lay church leadership but also provides a negative role model of Christian living for congregants. We believe that the integrity of the gospel they preach is damaged as well. Although each one of our lives and ministries matters to God and to the body of Christ, none of us is indispensable. As recipients of God's grace, we as pastors shouldn't have to earn God's approval or love by our dedication, success, or perfection as pastors and neither should our congregants!

The key to healthy ministry is a theology of embodied mutual interdependence. The heart of the 1 Corinthians 12 vision of the "body of Christ" is the affirmation that each of us finds our unique and lively vocations fulfilled only in the context of the interdependent needs and concerns of the community of the faithful we serve. We all need each other. Our life actions shape not only each other's lives, but the life of our community and, ultimately, the well-being of our good, green earth. As cocreators with God we can and should rejoice in healthy teamwork among lay and clergy leadership and the spirit of Christ moving freely in our midst. At the same time, we can and should recognize the freedom implied in such interdependent teamwork. No one is absolutely essential all the time!

We rejoice that the lay leadership at Disciples United Community Church, where we pastor, is fully capable of preaching and leading worship in our absence. It is with great intentionality that we proclaim that each member of the congregation is a minister. We are merely the pastors of the congregation, called to equip and teach lay persons the many ways to embody their gifts in the body of Christ. During our recent emergency absences following our son's diagnosis of cancer, our hearts were soothed to know that the congregation would pull together and congregational life would go on superbly without us. Pastors who act as if they alone are essential to bringing about God's realm in their congregations lack basic trust in the omnipresent and omni-active God, who constantly calls forth lay persons and colleagues in our community to grow and flourish anew in their pursuit of God's vision of shalom—healing and wholeness, justice, beauty, and truth.

Divine leadership shares, rather than hoards power! The best thing we can do as pastors is simply "get out of the way." God's own Sabbath rest invites us to give ourselves and others plenty of space to become God's willing partners in healing the world and healing ourselves!

Healthy theology is manifested in healthy ministry. As prayerfully hospitable partners with God in healing ourselves, our congregants, and the world, we wish to lift up three main aspects of God's call to healthy, renewed, and renewing ordained ministry and congregational leadership:

1. *Every pastor has many callings, or vocations, and not just her or his pastoral call.* Each of our life responsibilities is connected with a lively and dynamic calling to live out our own lives within a healthy and robust web of relationships beginning first of all with our embodied self as it is interdependently related to our spiritual and emotional lives; then our family, our wider denomination and community, our nation, and last but not least our ecological stewardship of this planet and its human and natural resources. The shape and importance of each call fluctuates over time, but to ignore any set of relationships in this web is to ultimately damage our pastoral call.

2. *Within healthy congregational life, every person, and not just the pastor, is given many invitations, or calls, to be faithful to God in her or his own unique ways.* Visionary pastoral leadership awakens persons to seeing God's many visions for their lives and their own ministerial calls towards personal and planetary healing and wholeness. A visionary pastor affirms the universality of call and seeks to let go of power, modeling what it means for persons to be healthy, caring, and committed partners with others in God's reign of justice and shalom. The spiritually empowered and empowering pastor recognizes that her or his calling as congregational pastor is not *always* the most important call in her or his congregation.

3. *Vitally dynamic pastoral calls are lively and constantly changing.* While we are called to make many long-term commitments in our lives, such as the call to ordained pastorates, marriage, or other familial partnerships, even these calls change over time and are best lived out in the context of the freshness of God's renewed and renewing activity in each moment. Newness and novelty are good things. Maintaining the status quo is nowhere in the Bible lifted up as a virtue of inspired and inspiring leadership!

Having a vital, dynamic sense of one's personal and professional callings involves openness to the ever-changing interplay between God's calls and our responses in the everyday events of our lives. A lively theological vision of pastoral call invites us and our congregants to creativity and responsibility amidst prayerful hospitality for one another's gifts. We are invited to remember that the grace of this theological vision is that we are not alone and that we have many partners in God's realm whose gifts we need to affirm and receive in order to best actualize our own vocations in ministry.

Yes, God's call may still challenge us, at times, to long days and long nights of labor, but these long days and nights are not to be spent in over-functioning workaholism, but in "working out our salvation with fear [awe] and trembling [care]," that is, in prayerful discernment about how and where we are called to be faithful in our many partnerships in healing the earth and bringing justice and hope to our communities. Our great joy in ministry is found too in the deeper grace that calls us to play, rest, re-create, honor our families, and even accept our failures as part of God's larger holy adventure! We can take a Sabbath and trust that God will continue to call others to faithful leadership, "for it is God who is at work in you; enabling you both to will and work for God's good pleasure." (Phil. 2:13) Could God be calling you as an overworked and overcommitted pastor to "consider the lilies": to feast your eyes on the beauty of your life partners, children, or animal companions, to rejoice in the sunset or leap happily from your bed to greet the new day proclaiming, "This is the day that God has made! I rejoice and give thanks in it!"? What would it look like for you to embrace, right now, this call to be a good steward of your embodiment? Could it be that the Holy Spirit is calling you to be a better steward of your embodiment and your life's many callings in addition to your call as an ordained pastor? How can you best fulfill your vocation to "shine like stars in the world" (Phil. 2:15) and become more aware of God's bright grace that refreshes and inspires each moment of your life?

THE PAUSE THAT ENERGIZES

In the midst of a time of upheaval, God through the psalmist invites God's community to "be still and know that I am God! I am exalted among the nations, I am exalted in the earth." God's call to stillness helps us to take a spiritual and physical holy-day, even if only for a short period of time, trusting that "the Lord of hosts is with us; the God of Jacob is our refuge" (Psa. 46:10–11). Our work will get done even if we take half an hour a day for silent contemplation or meditation. Because the whole world is truly in God's hands, we can take time to care for the small part of the world that is our *primary* responsibility—our own physical, emotional, mental, and spiritual well-being—that in turn enables us to bring joy and beauty to our families and communities.

A vital, renewed, and renewing ministry depends a good deal on our particular theological perspective as it relates to the meaning of our lives and vocation. Listen to the words of Psalm 8:

> O [God], our Sovereign,
> How majestic is your name in all the earth!
> You have set your glory above the heavens. . . .
> When I look at your heavens, the work of your fingers,
> the moon and the stars that you have established;
> what are human beings that you are mindful of them,
> mortals that you care for them?
> Yet you have made them a little lower than God,
> and crowned them with glory and honor. (Psa. 8:1, 3–5)

Vital, renewed, and renewing ministry is grounded in trusting God's wisdom, gradually and steadily working in the heavens above and in the intricacies of our own physiology. Our job is simply to open ourselves to it and allow its ordering, re-creative potentials into our lives.

In our clergy nurture groups we encourage pastors to take time to meditate on photographs of the universe taken by the Hubble telescope and in a similar spirit of awe-full appreciation, to study books on the wonders of our physical bodies and their intricate construction. Filled with awe and appreciation, we are inspired to love the universe in all its grandeur and at the same time love more deeply the mortal flesh that is our own unique revelation of God, revealing in every cell the movements of divine care and wisdom.

In the first chapter, we invoked the psalmist's affirmation, "let everything that breathes praise God" (Psa. 150:6). What would it mean for you to put down this book and breathe in God's wonder right now? What about taking similarly spirited "wonder-full breaks" in the midst of your workday? What visual aids would help you to do so? Kate has a photograph of earth broadcast back from a space exploration vehicle on the other side of Saturn as her screensaver on her computer. Saturn with all its gaseous rings fills the foreground, and earth is but a tiny speck in the distance peeking in between the rings. Whenever she sees this screensaver Kate is filled with praise for the greatness of the God's creative powers throughout the universe, and she feels awe for the exciting journey of humans to explore and understand them! She says, "My own life and loves are put into perspective too. They seem at once very small and yet also very great. 'What are human beings that you are mindful of them, mortals that you care for them?'"

GLORIFYING GOD IN OUR BODIES

As God's beloved creations, we reflect the embodied wisdom that was present in the incarnation of Jesus the Word and Wisdom of God. With Mother Teresa, we are called to "do something beautiful for God" and that includes our care of our bodies as well as our care of the earth and quest for justice and equality. Transforming our bodies, and moving from disease to wholeness in our physical lives and ministerial practice, is a matter of regularly following simple practices of healing and wholeness as best we are able. Such practices include not only prayerful awareness of our breathing but awareness of the holiness of our lives and all life while eating, while moving, through healing touch, and through healing rhythms of rest and activity.

The Hebraic scriptures tell the story of the encounter of Naaman, a foreign general suffering from leprosy, with Elisha the Hebrew prophet. When the prophet suggests the simplest of remedies, dipping seven times in the nearest river, the Jordan River, Naaman is incensed because he expected something expensive and complicated, worthy of his social standing. Despite his initial anger, he chooses to follow the prophet's remedy when his servants remind him that pathway to healing is right in front of him. "Father, if the prophet had commanded you to do something difficult, would you not have done it? How much more, when all he said to you was 'Wash, and be clean'?" (2 Kings 5:1–14). The pathway to embodied wholeness is right in front of us. Embodying God's desire for our healing and wholeness, regardless of our past behavior or current physical challenges, requires us simply to be mindful about following everyday healthy practices of diet, movement, touch, and rest. In these activities we are asked to have the same care and compassion for ourselves that we have for others. God wants us to be well and has placed the keys to wholeness in the most obvious place of all: simple, intentional, activities of everyday embodied life.

Holy Eating

Of the seven deadly sins, it is our experience that gluttony is one of the greatest temptations in our own and others' ministry. Most of our congregational and denominational gatherings and home visitations involve eating. To be sure, abundant and welcoming eating is one of the signs of vital congregational life. In the wake of Pentecost, the Jerusalem Christian community joined worship, study, and table fellowship:

> Day by day, as they spent much time together in the temple; they broke bread at home and ate their food with glad and generous hearts, praising God and having the good will of all the people. (Acts 2:46–47)

It is no coincidence that Jesus as a healer also transformed persons by inviting them to share in a radically inclusive table that welcomed all persons as God's beloved children, especially those who were perceived by the social and religious communities as sinful and unclean. Eating a meal together was and is an incredibly intimate, bonding experience. While table fellowship is gastronomical, it is also profoundly spiritual, relational, and emotional. A rural pastor, Tom recalls many afternoons in which he goes from farm to farm, drinking coffee and eating cookies and pie at each stop along the way. "If they love you, they feed you. I can't leave a home visit without a cup of coffee, and I mean high-test coffee, along with a cookie, piece of cake, or pie. It's like communion for my country congregation. With all that loving, I've gained thirty pounds in the past three years."

Sally describes her experiences at her congregation's potluck dinners, "When you're pastor, everyone's watching you at the potlucks. I have to take a little of everything just to be political. The women of the church always ask me, 'How did you like my cake? Did you enjoy my macaroni and cheese or shepherd's pie?' Even the few men who bring homemade dishes make a point of asking me if I tried their cake or covered dish. It is difficult even to take 'no thank you' helpings!"

What's a pastor to do in a church culture for which coffee hours and potlucks are primary social sacraments? How can a pastor be gracious in receiving hospitality, while eating a just and healthy diet? While New Testament theology challenges legalistic thinking of all kinds, Jesus' first followers saw eating as an ethical issue. "All things are lawful for me, but not all things are beneficial" (1 Cor. 10:23). Indeed, eating highly processed foods, also called eating "high" on the food chain, has profound ethical implications. Our North American weight problem is connected with poverty and starvation in the southern hemisphere. Our highly processed and high-caloric diets force southern hemisphere countries to focus on *our* needs for coffee and rich food, rather than the basic survival needs of their *own* people. Our health issues surrounding eating also affect the health and well-being of many people other than ourselves. Clearly, you can eat anything with anyone, and still be attuned with God. Nevertheless, what we eat and the ethics of food production and consumption are an important part of our overall spiritual, physical, emotional, and professional well-being. Our experience tells us that it is helpful to inform yourself about the social implications of your food sources, commerce, and processing, but hallowing your eating by only eating products that support a healthy, sustainable world is a very difficult task. For us this includes purchasing fair trade, organic, and local produce, including coffee, whenever possible. Still, there are no easy answers.

In general we recommend following standard nutritional guidelines. Recent medical studies indicate that the healthiest diets are low in refined carbohydrates, red meat, refined sugars, and artificial and processed ingredients. A healthy diet may include an abundance of fruits, vegetables, fish, some poultry, and organic, unprocessed foods. It is our experience, however, that it is also helpful to explore your dietary needs from an energetic and spiritual perspective. What foods enable you to feel lively and vital throughout the day? As a spiritual practice, we invite you to experiment with your current diet for a week or two. Without changing your diet, initially notice how you feel—physically, emotionally, and spiritually—following each snack or meal. Do you feel more energy or less? Is your mind clear or fuzzy? Do you take time to savor the taste of your meal or do you eat on the run? Then, if you sense that certain foods seem to drain your energy and vitality, you can experiment with eliminating them from your diet for a week or two and then notice whether or not you feel better. Besides nutrition and the pure joy of eating, notice also if your eating practices might not reveal deeper spiritual, relational, or psychological needs. Do you find yourself eating to respond to feelings of personal emptiness? Do you eat when you are depressed or under stress? Are you a "comfort" eater? If your unhealthy eating habits reflect deeper emotional, relational, or spiritual issues, you may choose to seek the counsel of a therapist or spiritual guide. Further, any major dietary change should be entered into in consultation with your health care provider.

We call this sort of eating with awareness "holy eating," and it has been our experience that it fosters vital, renewed, and renewing spirituality. What we eat and drink truly matters. While our society is good at providing "fast food," God calls us to provide "soul food" for ourselves and others. Awareness in eating also involves gratitude for the gifts of food and companionship.

Sandy ate with haste and inattention until one day she realized the grace of eating. "I never realized how many hands touched my food before it reached my dinner table. Now, as part of my table blessing, I remember farmers and ranchers, truck drivers and food handlers, store clerks and stockers. I am also becoming more aware of issues of justice related to the food and beverages I consume. I am now committed to fair trade coffee as a way of supporting the well-being of those who pick the coffee beans for my morning coffee. Knowing that much of the food I eat has been harvested by 'undocumented workers' here in the United States, I have become sensitive to protecting the rights of our nation's most vulnerable guests."

It is appropriate that our "holy eating" turns our attention beyond good flavor and nutrition to issues of justice and shalom as well as enhanced personal and professional energy. The prophet Amos once asserted that the wealthy will experience a "famine" of hearing the word of God because of their injustice toward impoverished farm workers (Amos 8:11–12). Do we blunt our sense of God's presence by the type the type of food we eat and the relationship of that food to the well-being of our vulnerable neighbors?

In order to experience God's calling at our dinner tables we would do well to follow Stephanie Paulsell's advice: "Every time we sit down to a meal, we should remember two things: that life is sustained by God and that there are many, beloved by God, who do not have enough to eat. Gratitude and solidarity, practiced over and over, three meals a day, ought to shape not only how we receive our nourishment but how we receive our neighbor as well."[2]

Spiritual Movement

Moving one's body can be a very simple but effective spiritual practice. Bruce has a crystal paperweight on his desk at Lancaster Theological Seminary inscribed with Augustine's words, *solvitur ambulando,* "it will be solved in the walking." A dear friend gave Bruce the paperweight because she knows how much he loves walking—not just for exercise, but as a holistic spiritual exercise. Every morning before sunrise, Bruce takes a two- to three-mile walk in our neighborhood in the western suburbs of Lancaster, Pennsylvania. As he speed-walks in the predawn solitude, Bruce practices his morning prayers by breathing deeply and visualizing divine energy and light filling his body, mind, and spirit. He then focuses on his intercessory prayer list and repeats various spiritual affirmations for himself as well. Later in the day, Bruce often prepares his sermons and lectures as he fast-walks through the beautiful grounds of Franklin and Marshall College, adjacent to the seminary. Bruce begins his walks with germinal ideas and usually returns to his seminary study with a complete mental outline of his sermon or lecture. Inspiration can definitely come through the vehicle of perspiration! We, Kate and Bruce, take a walk together each day during which tie we exchange thoughts and feelings about our personal and professional lives. Taking a daily walk together has been central to the long-term health of our marriage and our work together as pastors.

Victoria has also learned the art of prayer walking. After her morning cup of coffee, she race-walks through her urban Washington, D.C., neighborhood, listening to gospel music, symphonies, and jazz. At times, this United Methodist pastor slows her pace to admire the sun peeking through the Washington skyline. At other times, she takes a longer loop to include a walk on the Capitol Mall. "Walking each morning gives me perspective. Instead of waking up with headline news, I begin the day with music and prayer, and that sets the tone for the rest of the day—for the challenges of ministry in an urban environment."

For Stephanie, a United Church of Christ pastor in the Midwest, the breathing and postures of yoga help her unite body, mind, and spirit. Although yoga has its origins in Hinduism, Stephanie experiences yoga as a way of becoming aligned and energized with divine inspiration on a daily basis. Ste has even initiated a yoga class in her midwestern congregation. Her congregants are learning the relationship between God's generous revelation in other religious traditions and their own personal health and well-being. In the spirit of the Logos theologians of the early church, they are discovering that wherever truth and healing are found, God is its source, even in the movement of our bodies.

Kate enjoys early morning body prayers, which are more akin to dance than exercise. With these movements she also enjoys singing a variety of chants that she learned from her spiritual director Isabella Bates at the Shalem Institute in Bethesda, Maryland.[3]

No one set of movements or exercises fits everyone. Joy and fitness are essential aspects of every healthy exercise plan. Just as our personality type shapes our style of work and recreation, our age, current physical condition, spiritual orientation, and personality type are essential factors in discerning the types of physical activities that will best enhance our well-being over the long haul. Whether you walk in your neighborhood or on the treadmill in front of the television, do aerobic exercises or Pilates at the health club, jog or walk around your neighborhood, or practice yoga, Tai Chi, or Qi Gong, you must experience joy in your exercise practice in order to have it spiritually sustain you over the long haul. John likes to run because of the "runner's high" he experiences as he races through his neighborhood. Cynthia enjoys swimming because in those thirty minutes of cutting through the water, she says, "I experience complete solitude. There are no cell phones or e-mails to answer. There are no pastoral emergencies that can disturb me." Maria walks with another woman pastor three times a week because "during that hour, we share our challenges of ministry, laugh at our reactions to certain pastoral situations, and take time simply to be still and notice the beauty of nature."

Surely, movement is the key to health and wellness, but we would like you to also consider that it may be the key to understanding God's life as well. One translation of God's response to Moses' question about God's identity reports that response as "I am what I will become" or "I am becoming" (Exod. 2:14). As we move, we align ourselves with God's own lively movements in our lives and in the world. Our God is a God of wind and fire who honors the past, but never stands still. Our God is a God of creative process, always in motion. This same God calls *us* to rhythms of rest and motion of mind, body, and spirit.

Healthy pastors experience the integration of spirituality and healing as they share in God's movements by walking, swimming, dancing, jogging, yoga, Tai Chi, and other forms of dynamic exercise. In dynamic movement, these pastors experience their minds, bodies, and spirits opening more fully to divine energy and inspiration, and they find new vitality for the challenges of ministry. New ideas emerge, old habits are released, and new possibilities are envisaged. Like Eric Lidell, the Scottish pastor-runner of *Chariots of Fire* fame, we can experience God's pleasure in our walking, running, jogging, swimming, or yoga exercises. This divine delight gives us energy for the journey of ministry.

Healing Touch

In the biblical tradition, touch confers God's blessing and mediates God's healing presence. Jesus' touch transforms persons' lives in a myriad of ways, awakening God's healing power within them, restoring the divine wholeness that had been hidden by disease, and welcoming them into God's realm. In touching social outcasts, Jesus overcomes dualisms of saved and sinner, healthy and sick, welcomed and ostracized. Jesus' touch enables persons to experience God's abundant life in mind, body, spirit, and healing.

So, too, vital, renewed, and renewing ministry is nurtured and sustained by appropriate and sacred touch. While in the context of our professional lives, caring touch must be dispensed with the same care as pharmacists dispense medications. Genuinely loving touch can truly heal and transform. Because of the reality of widespread pastoral misconduct, we believe that too much emphasis has been put on negative aspects of touch. Yes, unhealthy touch can wound and traumatize the spirit as well as the flesh, but we believe that well-boundaried, welcome, and loving touch can restore relationships, heal emotions, enliven the spirit, and support God's gentle healing of persons traumatized by sexual, physical, or psychological abuse. Recognition of the intricate interdependence of embodiment helps pastors to honor and creatively embrace the weaving together of mind, body, spirit, emotions, memories, and hopes in every touch and every word. In everyday ministry, we have experienced the transforming and supporting power of a healthy hand clasp or "A frame" hug during the "exchange of peace" in nurturing our own and others' wellness.

Touch grounds us in God's good earth, joining us with others in God's dynamic and interdependent world. The biblical stories of the first human couple as well as the love poems of the Song of Songs reveal God's lively eros toward beauty within our own lively, erotic, and intimate relationships. Touch is the visible sign of God's love within our loves. "Naked and unashamed," we experience our bodies as a sacred gift, whether we are infants or octogenarians. Through touch, we are, as Stephanie Paulsell notes, awakened to our "sacred vulnerability," the fragile interdependence within which we live and move and have our being.[4]

Because touch is moral and spiritual in nature, we must always "handle with care." John Naisbett, author of *Megatrends*, asserts that in the midst of technological advances, we need to balance "high-tech" with "high-touch" whether in medical settings or our own personal and professional lives. For pastors, touch should never be "dispensed" casually or in a way that is at all invasive of personal space. Precisely because touch is a central medium of divine incarnation and healing, we are called to the highest level of care in touching others. We must also see to it that we nurture our own quality experiences of healing touch for ourselves through appropriate channels such as therapeutic massage, reiki healing touch, or healthy social or familial relationships. It is when pastors ignore or repress their own healthy needs for touch that they unconsciously (and sometimes even consciously) foist their own needs for touch inappropriately upon congregants.

Our faith and practice as pastors are nurtured and sustained by intimate and holy relatedness with the earth, loved ones, and professional colleagues. If we are to reclaim the mantle of the prophet, shaman, and healer, we need to reclaim our bodies as vehicles for revelation by God. But, sadly, many pastors are disconnected from their divine embodiment. Alienated from their bodies, they become dissociated "talking heads" whose disembodied words deaden worship services and drain congregations of the vital energies they need to transform the world. We believe that pastors, like their parishioners, need healing of the whole person, body, mind, spirit, and lively interpersonal relatedness, if they are to give light and warmth to others in their ministerial practice. Our words need to become flesh, as the glow of God's spirit arises from the flesh that embraces and shapes it.

Sharon discovered the healing of her embodiment through the healing touch of massage therapy. Stressed out and near brownout, Sharon found herself floating through the day, spiritually and physically disconnected from herself, her family, and her congregants. According to Sharon, "my theology seemed disembodied and irrelevant, until I experienced God's healing touch in the hands of a massage therapist. For an hour twice each month, as I simply received the blessing of her touch, I experienced God's grace and restoration. Now, I'm once more connected with my body, the earth, my congregation, and family. My spirit is restored."

Basically shy, despite his success in ministry, Michael completely refrains from hugging congregants. Therefore, he bathes in the hugs that he gives and receives in his Lancaster Theological Seminary ministerial colleague group. "I feel God's presence in the intimacy of this group, where I can share my deepest feelings, hear others' stories of despair and hope in ministry, and then connect with healing embraces. For me, this is the word made flesh."

As a massage therapist and reiki practitioner and teacher, Kate integrates reiki healing touch in her spiritual direction with pastors as they struggle to find relief from the stresses of ministry. Grounded in the interplay of East and West, reiki healing touch is "prayer with your hands," awakening the practitioner and recipient alike to God's healing energy flowing through them. Many pastors simply need to relax and receive, to be "off duty" and let go of control for an hour in order to truly experience God's grace anew in their lives.

A seasoned reiki master/teacher and practitioner, Bruce enjoys teaching pastors how to give themselves reiki treatments. Bruce integrates self-reiki into his daily spiritual practice of centering prayer and walking prayer as yet another way of opening to God's abundant life-energy. As one who is constantly percolating creative programmatic, writing, and workshop ideas, Bruce experiences his own self-reiki treatments as a time to simply rest in God's energy and let God renew and revive his body, mind, and spirit. Often, as Kate has been quick to inform him, Bruce falls asleep during his own self-reiki treatments, simply resting in God's renewing and re-vitalizing grace.[5] Kate, in contrast, gives herself reiki primarily when she is "on the go" and needs to pause and spiritually center herself before a meeting or a pastoral visit.

We are persons of the earth as well as the sky. Healing touch enables us to experience our bodies as graceful, sacred, and loved, in every circumstance of life. Healthy touch awakens us to our connectedness with God's grace of embodiment and the beauty and power of caring relationships.

The Rhythm of Rest and Action

Peter notes that when he began in ministry, he needed to work nonstop to grow the church and minister to needy persons. "I was always on duty. I slept, but I went to sleep thinking of the next day's appointments, and I awakened thinking of my pastoral tasks right through my quick shower and coffee and toast before dashing off to my first appointment. I was in love with ministry, but soon I realized that I was becoming tired of it as well! I woke up weary and went to sleep bone tired. I was late to everything. One day, I realized that if I didn't slow down, I might begin to make poor decisions or fail to appropriately respond to an important pastoral need. I suspected that I might burn out within in a matter of months." With this new realization, Peter began a slow but steady process of personal and professional transformation. He sought out a spiritual director, joined a colleague group for new pastors, began to exercise, and began a new routine of morning and evening prayer and recreation. "I discovered that I needed rest to maintain my ministry. Today, I take time for at least seven hours of sleep. I begin the day in prayer and study, and end the day with prayer and a good book. I go into the office an hour later but I am able to accomplish more work and I feel better about what I do. Now, I go to bed with a sense of peace and awaken ready to take on the challenges of ministry one step at a time."

God's evolving universe, always seeking harmony and balance, healing and wholeness, reveals a dynamic interplay between order and novelty, tradition and transformation, structure and chaos, rest and activity. We have discovered that the same dynamic can flourish in our lives as we seek to join the insights of the Hebraic tradition, in which the new day begins at sundown, with the Western notion of the day beginning in the morning with action—with quick preparations for the novelty of the new day and the challenge to change the world! We begin each day at home in the evening, preparing to rest and let go of responsibility for the world. Each day's adventure begins with rest, dreams, and silence that remind us, as they did Jacob, that "God is in this place." Vital, renewed, and renewing ministry involves a dynamic and creative balance between activity and receptivity, work and rest, creation and contemplation, words and silence.

Jesus' ministry reflected an awareness of this dynamic balance in everyday life. Recognizing the significance of rest in restoring his own and his followers' ministerial vitality, Jesus invited the disciples "to come away to a deserted place and rest awhile" (Mark 6:31) following their first teaching ventures on their own.

Balance is not a concept that pastors often think about and the fact is that we have found many pastors to be out of balance physically, intellectually, relationally, and spiritually. Because they are tired from an overabundance of projects, tasks, visits, and meetings, this lack of balance between rest and activity shows up in lackluster sermons, half-hearted administrative problem solving, absent-minded pastoral care, and unproductive meetings, not to mention a sense of detachment or distance from family members and significant others. Pastors need the gentle restoration that comes from resting in the rhythms of God's grace, protection, and energy. While there is no *one* rhythm of rest and activity for all persons, we suggest that pastors intentionally take time for receptivity and rest throughout the day, beginning with a period of quiet preparation for sleep (without the TV on) and getting enough sleep to begin the day with energy. Later in the day, we encourage pastors to practice some form of contemplative prayer, which roots their lives in divine inspiration and grace. For some activist pastors, engaging in centering prayer, journaling, or prayer shawl knitting may not be as helpful as merely taking time for a "power nap" or other restorative activity at the first signs of fatigue or as a preventative measure on the busiest days. While we cannot predict the moments when we will be called into action as pastors, we can prepare for the anticipated and un-expected demands of ministry by intentionally taking time for quiet mo-ments of "prayerful hospitality" to God, which we can then "pay forward" to others.

While we cannot manage time or ministry, we can take responsibility for shaping our days with regularly spaced times for prayer, relaxation, recreation, and relationship throughout the day and by claiming more sub-stantial time for spiritual growth, rest, and recreation each week. With Naaman, pastors need to remember that what we need to become whole is usually right in front of us, requiring only the effort of taking time to be mindful about our lives and ministry. When pastors protest that they "don't have time" for self-care or physical renewal or that "self-care is self-indul-gence," we respond by reminding them that they preventively service their automobiles and heating and air conditioning systems on a regular basis, even when they are running well!

FEEDING THE MINISTERIAL FIRE

The moment you sincerely say "yes" to God's questions—"Do you want to be made well? Do you want to feed the fire of wholeness and to embody vitality, spirituality, and health in your ministry?"—new pathways towards wholeness begin to emerge. With Naaman, you will discover practices of wholeness that have always been available to you. With God's wind at your back, you will discover simple practices of spiritual embodiment within the complexity of your ministry. You will, almost "magically," but really gracefully, discover that you have all the time you need to take care of your body and spirit as well as practice the arts of ministry with faith-fulness and excellence.

A Holistic Spiritual Formation Exercise

Once again, we suggest that our breathing is at the heart of healthy, en-ergetic, and transformative ministry. Surely, breath is at the heart of divine creativity and inspiration. God's spirit blows over the waters, and light, earth, and sea emerge. The Bible tells us that God breathes into clay and humankind awakens to its vocation of loving stewardship! Jesus breathes on his disciples, and they come alive, inspired to preach the good news of salvation and shalom. A mighty wind blows through Jerusalem on the feast of Pentecost, enlivening the first Christians for their ministry to the whole earth.

With prayerful, deep, and gentle breathing the simplest acts can become transformative. Through breath prayer, Deborah found a spiritual center that radiated divine energy into every aspect of her life and ministry, helping her to conquer feelings of hurry and anxiety. We observe that many pastors seem to be breathless, gasping for air when God wants to fill our lungs with healthy energy and love! Regardless of the terms we use to describe this breath of life—opening to God's spirit, *ruach, pneuma, chi,* or *prana*—we know that deeply and contemplatively embracing it awakens, revitalizes, energizes, and connects our every cell and every thought to the divine energy in whom we live and move and have our being.

Repetition grounds and deepens your spiritual practices in everyday life and so it is that no spiritual practice is easier to repeat than breath prayer (since you are constantly breathing, whether you are mindful of it or not!). The moment you begin breathing mindfully through centering prayer, guided visualizations, morning walking prayer, yoga, or any other form of mindful breathing that you enjoy, your whole body begins to relax and your mind becomes calm once more. The depths of your being will say "thank you" for your commitment to such moments of self-care and spiritual renewal.

So, once again, we invite you to simply breathe. Exhale any stress or weariness. Fill your lungs with each breath, visualizing God's Spirit filling you as you inhale. When you exhale, visualize yourself giving your stress and weariness to God. When your mind wanders, simply bring it back to God's healing and cleansing breath without judgment. Take three to five minutes at first. Later you may choose to practice this breathing meditation for twenty minutes once or twice a day.

Throughout your day, remember to breathe mindfully as you move from one task to another, as you pick up the phone, or as you prepare to make a pastoral call. Breathing mindfully through your ministerial tasks nurtures prayerful hospitality and reminds you that you are called to do only one thing amid the many tasks of ministry, and that is to mediate God's wholeness and salvation to everyone you meet.

A Practice for Healthy Ministry

We have found that healthy ministry is a matter of balance. In the "Tao" of ministry, the yin of contemplation gives depth to the yang of action and the yang of action gives meaning to the yin of contemplation.

We invite you to begin to practice balanced healthy ministry through a commitment to embodied self-awareness beginning with awareness of your breathing. Then throughout the week, practice becoming mindful of your body: How do you physically feel? Which one of your muscles is tight or sore? Do you feel cold and withdrawn or hot and overextended? How does your spiritual and relational life condition your sense of physical health? How does your diet influence your spiritual life, creativity, and ministerial focus? What foods bring you whole-person joy and leave you feeling satisfied and at ease physically? What foods contribute to weariness and fatigue of mind, body, and spirit?

If you currently do not have an exercise plan, what images of exercise awaken your desire to move with the spirit? After you choose a reasonable exercise plan, it is advisable to consult with your physician or nurse practitioner in order to see if this is the "right" practice for you, given your health condition. Begin slowly and gently with your new exercise plan. Don't overdo it! Walk, swim, or take an introductory class in yoga or aerobics simply for the joy of it. Do you experience God's pleasure? Do you experience your own intrinsic "natural high" from your increased cardiopulmonary circulation? Are new insights coming to you as you immerse yourself in holy motion? (If not, then search for another movement that you really *do* enjoy!)

An Affirmation of Faith

Do you experience your body as an enemy or hindrance, rather than a companion or friend? Do you feel inferior to the "ideal" male and female models you see in the media? Are you experiencing frustration or despair because of long-term neglect of your physical well-being? Are you aware of carrying the emotional and physical effects of abuse during childhood or trauma in the course of your professional life? Despite these realities of your life, remember that you still are God's beloved child and your body still reflects God's wisdom and care. Without denying your past experiences or your current health conditions, we invite you to consider practicing these life-transforming physical affirmations (or something similar of your own creation):

- My body is healthy and beautiful (while looking in the mirror each morning). I choose to eat foods that energize my body, mind, and spirit (while grocery shopping or standing in front of your refrigerator).

- God's spirit energizes me with every breath (while walking out of your door each morning).

A Covenant of Wholeness and Vitality in Ministry

While wholeness is a matter of the dynamic interplay of many factors— heredity, lifestyle, family of origin, environment, spirituality, our prayers and the prayers of others, God's gentle movements of grace in our lives— the fact is that health and healing are also a choice. When you say "yes" to God's vision of health for your life, new energy and purpose immediately flow to your life. Your physical condition reflects an implicit or explicit covenant with God and yourself. Take time, now, to create your own very intentional covenant for wholeness and vitality. You may want to make commitments similar to the following:

- I promise to take care of my body through healthy eating, exercise, rest, and holistic spiritual practices.

- I promise to glorify God by committing my life to healing and wholeness for myself and others.

- I promise to learn about and pursue justice for the vulnerable through what I eat as well as social and political advocacy.

THREE

TRANSFORMING YOUR MIND

In describing the new life that we experience when we respond to God's surprising grace, the apostle Paul affirms the unity of body, mind, and spirit in the Christian journey of salvation and wholeness. "Present your bodies as a living sacrifice, holy and acceptable to God, which is your spiritual worship. Do not be conformed to this world, but be transformed by the renewing of your minds, so that you may discern what is the will of God— what is good and acceptable and perfect" (Rom. 12:1–2). Faithfulness to Christ, Paul asserts, embraces the totality of our lives and requires a commitment to integrating intellectual, spiritual, and physical well-being.

For pastors, practicing creative intellectual transformation must involve more than just tackling the *New York Times* crossword puzzles to keep up our mental agility as we age! We are called to explore new ways of understanding God, the world, the culture in which we live, and our congregations. Continually maturing theological reflection is about actively loving

God with your mind with a foremost value on being transformed, seeing "through God's eyes" and imagining God's future shining brightly with new possibilities for yourself and others. As we reflect on our current theological visions and interpretations of God's activity in the world, we are called, with the twelve-year-old Jesus, to grow in "wisdom and stature" (Luke 2:52). Our vision of God, the universe, and human potential (our own included) needs to be revised constantly in order to keep up with God's dynamic movements in our lives and congregations.

For those spiritual adventurers willing to ride the rapids of our "permanent whitewater" postmodern world, the challenge is how to "keep your paddle down ready for contact with water," as one whitewater rafting guide once instructed Kate, even if your raft is bouncing swiftly through the air, and all the while be looking around to discern the calmest passage of water ahead toward which to steer! No easy task to be sure! Quantum physics, process theology, and systems theory suggest that the appearance of stable, fixed entities and ways of doing things is at best an illusion. Once one realizes that all is in flux, the challenge is to discern patterns of beauty and order amidst the chaos. The consolation given us by quantum physics is that these patterns of beauty and order *do* exist amidst the chaos and that we can indeed align ourselves and the energies of our communities with these energies, if we are able to train our eyes and our imaginations to see them! In the spirit of philosopher Alfred North Whitehead, this means that pastors are challenged to embody *creative* as well as *adaptive* leadership, that is, to initiate novelty to match the novelty of the environment and, moreover, to continually open their imaginations to see the many creative possibilities that are on the horizon for our congregations and communities.

Following Craig Dykstra's image of the "pastoral imagination," a unique and creative way of interpreting the world through the lenses of ministerial vocation and faith, pastors must, first of all, be imaginative, that is, be willing to entertain concrete and insightful alternatives to the current values and norms of their communities and congregations. To be sure, this is a tall order for any pastor, who must preach regularly, address the many/mini crises of building and institutional management, and respond sensitively to pastoral needs of congregants. For twenty-first-century North American pastors, the call to live by a different vision of this world requires looking beyond current parochial norms in congregational, denominational, and community life. It involves embracing continual personal and corporate transformation as essential to pastoral leadership and congregational vitality. It also requires an explicitly named and embraced faith in a God who is *not* the enforcer of the status quo, but instead, the source and inspiration for all novelty and growth. Vital ministry in the permanent whitewater world leaves no room for complacency. Complacency can only lead to stagnation and death.

In her book *An Interrupted Life*, Etty Hellisum, who died in a Nazi concentration camp, expresses her quest to become a "thinking heart." As pastors who are committed to a life of continual intellectual and spiritual transformation, we are also called to become "thinking hearts" as we seek to embrace the "mind of Christ" as persons committed to holistic thinking and living, keeping in mind always the greater good of the whole. Author Madeleine L'Engle, in her time trilogy, portrays the source of evil in the cosmos in terms of a disembodied mind, a mind disconnected from the concrete realities of flesh and blood and environmental context. By contrast, the mind of Christ embraces the joy and the pain of the world through compassionate imagination. Not content to dwell in the splendor of abstract and disembodied divinity, vital, renewed, and renewing pastors creatively embrace the truth that the word of God can become flesh in each of us just as it did in the healer and teacher of Nazareth. We can rejoice in the truth that if the revelation of God in Jesus of Nazareth was able to arise from the flesh, the womb of humble Mary and life in the carpenter's shop, then it can guide and transform our lives too.

Jesus' own "prophetic imagination," to use the language of Walter Brueggemann, was rooted in his lively and creative encounters with outcasts, disenfranchised women, disfigured lepers, and aimless and unfulfilled religious leaders and business persons. So, too, can ours. Jesus' healing ministry—and all of Jesus ministry, even his controversies with the religious leaders—was aimed at healing and transformation. It involved seeing wholeness and beauty where others saw disfigurement, disability, and impurity. Jesus saw something holy and vital in those to whom he ministered, and Jesus' affirming, imaginative vision of others helped them to take action in their lives in line with their stature as God's beloved, vital, and creative children.

One of Bruce's teachers, Bernard Loomer, described "stature" as the ability to embrace as much reality as possible without losing your personal center. According to Loomer, "by size I mean the stature of a person's soul, the range and depth of his [or her] love, his [or her] capacity for relationships. I mean the volume of life you can take into your being and still maintain your integrity and individuality, the intensity and variety of outlook you can entertain in the unity of your being without feeling defensive or insecure." The mind of Christ is constantly growing in wisdom and in stature, in the ability to experience God in all things and all things in God.[1] Stature is the gift of deep listening to yourself as well as others. In what sorts of new activities might you engage to increase your stature—your fullest embrace of "the mind of Christ" in your ministry? Nurturing your own emerging intellectual and emotional wholeness will allow you to have greater spiritual fortitude in helping others to become whole, on God's terms and not your own.

If stature involves experiencing the full range of your intellectual and emotional life, while holding in "prayerful hospitality" diverse theological and political positions and looking for value in viewpoints with which you disagree, where and with whom might you explore value in viewpoints with which you disagree? For example, in a world in which progressives and fundamentalists question each other's spiritual and theological authenticity, a person of stature will seek to understand the deeper meaning of Christian fundamentalism while still holding gently to her or his own more progressive vision of reality with integrity and grace. What would it require for you to enter into dialogue with a congregant or colleague who is much more conservative than yourself and try to discover shared values, rather than to defeat or convert that person?

The philosopher Gottfried Leibniz once suggested that philosophical systems err more in what they deny than what they affirm. Accordingly, what would it look like for you to affirm the virtues of the "old time religion," while also honestly confessing your own more liberal or progressive bias in a nonthreatening way? As thinking hearts, we invite you to experiment with such encounters, explore areas of common ground, and grow to appreciate the faithfulness of those with whom you disagree.

We believe that a vital, renewed, and renewing pastoral leadership is grounded in a commitment to holy relationships and emerging visions, rather than unquestioned and ungrounded theological assumptions. Embodied in the world of diverse relationships, complex family and congregational systems, and quickly changing social and environmental contexts, a pastor of stature with an imaginative transformed and transforming mind will see possibilities within limitations and will trust that "a way will be made when there is no way."

HEALING THE MIND

Physicians and other healers have always known that the mind is an important factor in physical health and illness. Pharmaceutical companies employ the placebo effect in medical trials. A placebo is a medically useless substance with which positive benefits are associated; for example, a sugar pill can relieve arthritis or lower blood pressure if the patient believes in its efficacy. Researchers have found that placebos work remarkably well in pain relief and the reduction of symptoms. On the other hand, researchers have also noted the "nocebo" effect, the impact of negative beliefs on our health and wellness. When they are told that a medication has negative side effects, patients often experience these same symptoms, despite the fact that the medication has no medical value. So it is that our beliefs, expectations, and systems of thought contribute to health or disease of body, mind, and spirit. Just think of the last time you were around a person with an itchy rash of unknown origins and then began to feel itchy yourself!

We have repeatedly affirmed that Jesus' ministry of healing was holistic. It joined spiritual, emotional, physical, and intellectual healing. As a leader who inspired faith and trust, Jesus awakened God's healing presence in persons experiencing illness. Recall, if you will, what the woman with the flow of blood says to herself over and over as she comes toward Jesus, "If I but touch his clothes, I will be made well" (Mark 5:28). Before God's healing energy has actually flowed from Jesus into her life, her faith has already opened the door of her heart and mind to God's healing power. Jesus acknowledges the role of her faith as a factor in the healing process with words of blessing and affirmation when he says, "Daughter, your faith has made you well; go in peace, and be healed of your disease" (Mark 5:34).

The healing of Jairus' daughter, within which the narrative of healing of the woman with the flow of blood is found, suggests that the beliefs of a community are a significant factor in healing and illness and life and death (Mark 5:21–24, 35–43). When the mourners deny the possibility that this twelve-year-old can be brought back to wholeness, Jesus expels the naysayers from the house and invites only the parents and his closest disciples to accompany him to the girl's bedside. Jesus creates an affirming healing community of persons who are willing to believe that Jairus' daughter can be awakened from her coma.

Cognitive psychologists and professional life coaches emphasize the importance of identifying and challenging their clients' beliefs that place limitations on their ability and capacity to change. Beliefs can open the door to divine possibilities or confine us to the prison of past failures. During a challenging personal and professional time some years ago, Bruce trained as a facilitator of "attitudinal healing." Inspired by the work of Jerry Jampolsky and Susan Trout, Bruce began to renew his relationships and professional life by focusing on his deepest identity as a "child of light and power" through the use of healing affirmations and intentional practices of forgiveness. Our marriage relationship grew in leaps and bounds when we began to share in daily devotional practices adapted from a book by Susan Trout called *To See Differently.* The core practice was to choose to become a "love finder" rather than a "fault finder." Old limitations fell away as we discovered, first intellectually and then in every other aspect of our lives, that we could let go of the past and embrace God's open future with a greater sense of empowerment and self-awareness. We moved out of feeling like victims in our life's circumstances to claiming our responsibility as actors in shaping our less than fulfilling ministry and marital situations.[2] Bruce writes about his experiences in the context of his transformational devotional book, *The Power of Affirmative Faith,* which focuses biblical affirmations as a resource for personal and social transformation.[3]

Biblical texts are replete with positive devotional affirmations that can heal and transform both individuals and communities of faith. While you cannot change everything in your life through the daily use of affirmations, we believe that immersing oneself in healing and empowering affirmations during times of crisis and transition can be a major source of pastoral renewal and transformation. Reflect for a moment, if you will, on the kind of energy drain you experience when you hear someone in a congregational setting say, "But we've always done it that way!" Then take a moment to consider the self-limiting associations inherent in sentences that begin with "I can't . . ." or "I've never been good at . . ." or "I'll never be able to change the way I am." Think of how many children's lives you have seen stunted by parents, teachers, or coaches labeling them with images of worthlessness, inferiority, or passivity. What have you done to help yourself come out from under such stultifying negative influences in your life? What can you do to help others come out from underneath such limiting and destructive influences?

When Paul says, "Do not be conformed to this world, but be transformed by the renewing of your minds," he invites persons to let go of past limitations and embrace more fully God's vision of our lives as beautiful, wonder-full, and gifted in so many ways. We invite you to pause a moment and consider the following questions: What negative statements or thought systems are currently limiting your personal and professional life? What self-images and self-talk are keeping you from experiencing God's abundant life right now (as a spouse or partner, parent, and pastor)? Where do you see your congregation living by negative or limiting images relating to worship and growth and how can you see yourself transforming them?

The heart of the gospel is the good news that "if anyone is in Christ, she is a new creation; if anyone is in Christ, he is a new creation." What would it mean for you to affirm that God is constantly seeking wholeness and shalom in every person you meet? What would it look like for you to actively affirm that God's world is an *open system* in which new possibilities and energies are always emerging? Claiming the power of God's grace through a lively commitment to affirmative faith can transform the conscious mind, filling it with life-changing images, and can awaken the healing powers of the unconscious mind as well. It can open us to greater physical well-being and empower us to innovative acts of relational, professional, and political healing and wholeness.

When we teach workshops or courses in pastoral leadership, we often ask participants to rephrase biblical affirmations in the first person. For example, after reading Matthew 5:14, "you are the light of the world," we ask the participants to repeat the affirmation, "I am the light of the world."

While these words seem arrogant or prideful to some, we remind them that Jesus is speaking these words to *all* of his followers and these same followers are admonished not to hide their lights under a bushel basket! (Matt. 5:15). If you don't believe that you are the light of the world—and everyone else is too—then by implication, you're calling Jesus a liar! If pastors don't let their lights shine before others, so that others may see their good works and give glory to God (Matt. 5:16), then who will?

Bruce counsels seminarians and novice pastors to take several deep breaths before they approach the pulpit and silently affirm, "God is speaking powerfully through me today! My sermon will benefit everyone who is listening." Think of the power inherent in Paul's words to the Philippians: "I can do all things through [Christ] who strengthens me" (Phil. 5:13) and "My God will fully satisfy every need of yours according to [God's] riches in glory in Christ Jesus" (Phil. 5:19). Remember that these life-changing affirmations of faith are preceded by Paul's invitation to positive spiritual formation practices:

> Finally, beloved, whatever is true, whatever is honorable, whatever is pure, whatever is pleasing, whatever is commendable, if there is any excellence and if there is anything worthy of praise, think about these things. (Phil. 5:8–9)

While our thoughts do not entirely create our reality as some "new age" spiritual leaders would suggest, clearly our beliefs, our self-talk, and repeated spiritual affirmations shape our attitudes, the way we experience the world, our sense of empowerment and efficacy, and our vision of possibilities. Healing the mind involves seeing yourself in the mirror of God's love and affirming yourself as God's beloved, competent, open-hearted, healing partner in every aspect of your life. To do so is not a denial of the concrete realities of past mistakes or of the limitations imposed by negative factors in our environment such as poverty, social discrimination or oppression, familial abuse or neglect, but a placing of these realities in the context of the larger realities of God's beneficent activity in our lives. Through faith we can embrace the many new possibilities given us by God in each moment. Jesus the healer invites us to let go of the negative power of the past and embrace God's new creation for ourselves and our congregations.

TRANSFORMING WORDS

Words are powerful tools for transformation. A regular component of our Lancaster Theological Seminary pastoral colleague group meetings is a time in which the participants share about a book that they have recently read. Excitement fills the room and faces begin to glow as pastors share about books that have changed their lives.

Meister Eckhardt once asserted that we are all "words of God." To be sure, as pastors, we are "people of the book" whose lives revolve around reading scripture, theology, and a wide range of literature and the arts. In the course of a lifetime of ministry, whether we preach from a manuscript, outlines, or extempore (memory) most of us generate the equivalent of two to three hundred pages of text a year and as many as ten thousand pages in a career!

Words can transform our lives, and yet pastors often fail to embrace this basic tenet of our faith in our own lives and ministries. While, on the one hand, most of us affirm that language of racism, sexism, and heterosexism clearly limits our lives and oppresses persons, we have not schooled ourselves as we ought in alternative language sets that transform and liberate us from limiting belief systems. Bruce remembers how his encounter with Paul Tillich's *Dynamics of Faith* enabled him to affirm that he could be a Christian, even though he could no longer ascribe to the sin-laden "orthodox" beliefs of his conservative Baptist childhood. Reading Alfred North Whitehead, John Cobb, and other process-relational theologians opened the door for Bruce to embrace a constructive and life-giving theological vision that inspired him to enter ministry and academic life as a theologian. Words become flesh as we learn new, life-enhancing ways to see ourselves, understand God, and relate to other persons.

While words are meant to be embodied, they are also meant to give us a vision of reality that inspires change in our daily lives and ameliorates the pain of human encounters with suffering, sickness, and death. As artists of the word, pastors need to read widely and reflect deeply. We suggest that every pastor have a dynamically evolving professional library that embraces the newest poetry, fiction, devotional reading, and theological reflection and that he or she establish regular times of immersion in the arts and music.

We are called to be artists of spirit, creating sacred encounters in word and deed through which our congregants can experience anew their own creativity, beauty, and truth. In our congregation last year, Kate and one of the lay leaders initiated an "Artist's Way" gathering group, using Julia Cameron's *Artist's Way* as its weekly inspiration. In this program, participants covenant to do their daily "morning pages," three pages of free-flowing writing, the creativity of which, unlike journaling, is valued primarily for its meditative process rather than its product. In addition participants are asked to take themselves on weekly "artist dates," which playfully and joyfully nurture their inner artist. Through this program, it is common for more than one participant to explore and pursue significant vocational and lifestyle changes. Others simply discover life-transforming imaginative and creative resources that they never knew they had. One pastor we know uses the daily stream of consciousness writing discipline that she learned in the *Artist's Way* as a means of liberating her from an overly critical inner "editor," which blocked her understanding of scripture and her creativity as a preacher. She notes, "Once I start writing, new ideas emerge as if from nowhere. But I know they come from God's Spirit within me."

Bruce teaches courses in spiritual autobiography in the doctor of ministry curriculum at Wesley Theological Seminary in which, in the spirit of Frederick Buechner and Parker Palmer, he invites participants to "listen to your life" and "let your life speak." Awakened anew to the depths of their personal experience, participants learn to see their lives as truly "holy adventures" in which divine surprises abound.

From this perspective, the discipline of preaching can be seen as a primary vehicle for personal transformation. As one pastor notes, "Where else would I have the opportunity to spend ten hours each week, immersing myself in scripture, exploring my encounter with God, and sharing God's good news?" Another pastor found preaching tedious until she connected it with her own intellectual and spiritual growth. "Now I see each week as one extended prayerful conversation with God. I have discovered that God is still speaking in my life and in scripture. I am blessed to experience and share my encounter with God forty-eight weeks of the year."

Even for those pastors who do not preach every week, preaching is an essential part of one's spiritual and intellectual formation. For example, associate and assistant ministers who may only preach once a month may find it enriching to use the lectionary for personal study and devotions even on the weeks when they are not preaching. In the concluding section on "feeding the fire within," we will outline a three-fold preaching practice that includes the use of *lectio divina*, imaginative prayer, and spiritual affirmations. This approach, along with a commitment to regularly absorbing the riches of diverse forms of literature and the arts, can bring life and energy to pastors in the pulpit and out.

The transforming mind nurtures the richness of words and images that flow to us and through us from a wide variety of sources including both the unconscious and the conscious mind. In truth, we are one whole being, dynamically synthesizing our embodiment, our minds, and our environment in every moment of experience. God speaks through our hopes and dreams, known and unknown, streaming through us and our "sighs too deep for words." A prolific writer, Bruce often asks God to awaken him to his unconscious mind as a resource for his writing. As he goes to sleep, he asks God for healing dreams, surprising insights, and creative solutions to problems. More often than not, he receives the guidance he needs. Kate trusts the insights that come to her through a lifetime of daily journal keeping and her intuitive dream interpretation, which is shaped by both gestalt and Jungian psychology. When we seek to grow in the mind of Christ, the whole universe can be a resource for creativity and personal transformation.

MOVING WITH THE SPIRIT

In our region of central Pennsylvania, local humor notes that some folks are afraid to cross the Susquehanna River to get back and forth from York to Lancaster. The truth is that many people rarely leave their rural county areas except to travel to Harrisburg or Philadelphia for medical care. While Alfred North Whitehead notes that spiritual and philosophical giants such as Jesus and Socrates surveyed the universe only from the narrow confines of Galilee and Athens, it has been our experience that travel is an essential part of broadening and transforming the mind. If God is everywhere, then revelation can happen anywhere, but the grandeur of divine revelation is more deeply witnessed by those who gaze upon the stars from distant mountaintops and hear God's wisdom spoken in different dialects. The power of

Paul's theology is his synthesis of different cultures. Unique in all of scripture, Paul's speech in the Athenian Areopagus combines the wisdom of a Stoic philosopher with Christian faith when he affirms that God is the reality in whom "we live and move and have our being" (Acts 17:28).

Travel or movement, whether by early Christians such as Paul and Thomas or the later Celtic Christians, is what enabled Christianity to become a global religion. It also enabled Christians to understand the Christ as a universal rather than merely a parochial or ethnic figure. While many Christians regret the synthetic relationship between Hebraic religion and Greek philosophy, some of the most inspiring and majestic passages of Wisdom literature and John's Gospel arose precisely because of the lively dialogue with the philosophical concepts of the surrounding Hellenistic culture. As they were able to imagine Jesus as the cosmic Christ, these early Christians were also able to discover the key to progressive Christian transformation, that wherever truth and healing are found, God is its source.

In Lancaster, Pennsylvania, after putting up a "for sale" sign on its church building, one local congregation announced on its placard, "the Spirit said move, and so we did!" Vital, renewed, and renewing ministry is grounded in the interplay of the micro and the macro that arises from weaving together awareness of the local community with diverse perspectives gained through travel throughout the nation and across the globe. This is why most seminaries include a cross-cultural immersion experience among their required curricula. Lancaster Theological Seminary students come back from Costa Rica, India, and South Africa with an expanded theological and experiential vision that adds stature to their studies and future ministries.

Recently a number of Lancaster Theological Seminary students and staff returned from taking high school students from the seminary's Leadership Now program on a journey through the borderlands between the United States and Mexico. Their images of "undocumented workers" and "illegal aliens" were transformed. Black and white statistics were transformed into God's beloved children. Upon returning from the trip, some participants even took to the streets to protest a speech by a political official who was advocating strict laws that they thought unfairly punished immigrants and their employers. Jimmy Buffet once sang "changes in latitudes, changes in attitudes," and this applies to the practice of transforming ministry as well. A local pastor in one of our ministerial excellence and spiritual formation groups noted how traveling to Africa awakened him to the riches as well as tragedies of a continent he had previously known only through the *National Geographic*. "My sense of superiority was lost as I prayed with African Christians and learned about indigenous African religion. I now realize that I am called to awaken my congregation to the gifts and needs of Africa. We have already begun a partnership with congregations in western Africa."

Vital ministry appreciates diverse ethnic, theological, liturgical, and linguistic expressions. It affirms and preaches a Christianity that is larger than the local congregation, denomination, or the United States. It listens to the voices of our neighbors in Canada and Mexico as well as across the globe as they describe our land and its gifts and challenges. A ministry of stature challenges narrow nationalism along with racism, sexism, and homophobia. Grounded in the first century affirmation "wherever truth exists, God is its source," vital and transformative pastors keep their eyes open for truth in all its diverse religious expressions. They seek a Christ for the cosmos, who is also as intimate as our next breath.

Lively ministry involves taking time apart for travel as well as retreat and contemplation. We encourage pastors to build their sabbaticals around both travel and study. International pulpit exchanges provide one such opportunity. Another low-cost travel opportunity open to pastors is to take members of their congregation on study tours or work trips to other countries or parts of North America. Through witnessing Christ in other cultures, we are better able to discern the many faces of Christ in our own neighborhood!

FEEDING THE MINISTERIAL FIRE

Seeking the mind of the cosmic Christ with a spacious, lively and curious mind is at the core of dynamic and vital ministry. As you practice transforming your mind, you are called to remember the intimate interdependence of mind and body. What nurtures the body enlivens the mind; what expands the mind enhances physical well-being.

A Holistic Spiritual Practice

Vital, renewed, and renewing ministry is the gift of a peaceful and renewed mind. We have found that wholeness of body, mind, and spirit can be promoted through the practice of centering prayer. Centering prayer, as taught by Basil Pennington and Thomas Keating, is, like breath prayer, a simple, repetitive practice involving the following steps:

1. Find a quiet undisturbed place in your home or church.

2. Sit in a comfortable position with your back straight and, ideally, your feet on the floor.

3. Take a moment for gentle breathing as you pray for God's presence in your life.

4. Begin your prayer by repeating a simple prayer word or image, such as "light," "love," "peace," "Jesus," "healing," "God," as way of focusing your mind and going deeper into your whole being. At times, you may simply experience a sense of nothingness or complete wordless rest in God's presence in your life.

5. If random thoughts or external noises intrude on your focus, simply notice and gently let go of them without judgment and return your attention to your prayer word.

6. To help you bring your awareness back into the room we suggest concluding your time with our Savior's Prayer or some other meaning-ful verbal prayer form.

Ideally, if one practices centering prayer for fifteen to twenty minutes twice each day, one experiences physical and emotional renewal equivalent to that of two hours of deep sleep. Bruce has been practicing various forms of centering prayer since 1970, when he learned Transcendental Meditation at Berkeley, California. Each morning, Bruce looks forward to a half hour of quiet centering prayer before his morning walk, coffee, and study time.

A Practice for Healthy Ministry

Our thoughts can bring either calm or stress into our lives. They can promote health and wholeness or disease and discomfort. Throughout the week, no-tice your thoughts and responses to various situations. Notice also your "self-talk." How often do you berate yourself for a mistake or judge yourself as somehow inferior or undeserving? What would it take for you to see yourself as a child of God worthy of love and stop your overcritical self-talk?

Whenever you find yourself making negative oral (or inner) statements about yourself, such as "I'm stupid," "I'm forgetful, I wonder if I have premature Alzheimer's," "I don't have time to pray or meditate," "My preaching is boring," pause and take time to entertain an alternative vision of yourself by repeating affirming statements such as "I am wise and wonder-full!" or "I remember important things," or "God's light shines in me and through my sermons!" or "I have all the time I need to do what is important in life." Be a prophet to yourself as you examine your own life and seek to embody Christ's "prophetic imagination." What alternative and life-giving visions of your personal, intellectual, relational, or professional life are you able to imagine right now? Kate invites her spiritual directees to draw pictures or symbols of their creative images to keep before them at the office or on their dresser mirror.

An Affirmation of Faith

Affirmations are central to practicing vital, renewed, and renewing ministry. In this section, we invite you to explore some general pastoral affirmations and, then, reflect on your use of scriptural affirmations in your preaching.

As you look at your life, where do you see yourself needing to affirm God's wisdom, care, and giftedness? Like searchlights, affirmations enable us to experience deeper realities about ourselves. While affirmations do not deny our imperfections, they place them in the larger perspective of God's image in our lives. You may wish to try repeating the following affirmations as you seek to transform and renew your mind in accordance with God's aim at personal and global transformation:

- I am a lively and insightful preacher (best posted behind the pulpit).

- I respond to crisis and conflict with peace and creativity (best posted in your appointment book).

- I lead worship with skill and effectiveness (best posted wherever you work on liturgical planning).

- I bring out the best in myself and others (best posted on the inside of your front door).

- Divine wisdom and insight flows through my life and into the lives of others (best posted inside your appointment book).

Affirmative preaching sees preaching as the inspiration for regular spiritual practice and uses affirmations to call yourself and your congregants to positive transformation. Affirmative preaching involves a consideration of some of the following spiritual practices as important elements in the ongoing process of preparing and delivering sermons:

1. *Creatively receptive contemplation*—Allow yourself extended periods of quiet, nondirected reflection (without expectation) to let the words of scripture gently "soak" into your soul before exploring biblical commentaries and lectionary helps.

2. *Lectio divina*, or holy reading, which comes from the Benedictine tradition of listening deeply to scripture by reading the passage over a few times (preferably out loud to yourself) in order to discern a particular word, sentence, or image that "leaps out at you" and calls you to a place of deep personal meaning for your life at this moment. You might, for example, take a "preaching walk" like Bruce does to join the creative movements of mind and body and spirit as you reflect on the meaning of a scriptural passage for your life and the life of your congregation. However you do it, take time to meditate on the word, phrase, or images that "leapt out at you" first, in terms of your own life and then, more broadly, in terms of the life of your congregation and the world.

3. *Imaginative prayer*, which comes from Ignatian spiritual practices— using your five senses to imagine the scene in the biblical narrative. Pause to notice the details of the scene, the other characters, the challenge at hand, and Jesus himself. Choose one character in the narrative to be the focus of your imaginative prayer. Become, in your mind's eye, that character. What do you look like? Are you employed outside of the house? What is the environment like? Who are your companions? What thoughts or feelings are going through your mind?

   In the course of your imaginative prayer, imagine yourself conversing with Jesus about your current life situation or a situation in your congregation. Does he touch or pray with you? What do you say to one another? What wisdom or healing does Jesus give you?

In the course of your sermon preparation, you may choose to also be another character in the narrative. Take time to notice the particular challenges of each character and the healing journey each must take.

A Covenant of Wholeness and Vitality in Ministry

Today's covenant is about expanding your consciousness of the world. You might start small by noticing the new buds or listening to the birds in your garden. Or, without hurry, let yourself be carried away by the carefree joy of the children playing in a nearby park. At other times you might take time to gaze up and try to identify the constellations in the night sky or the crystalline formations of ice and snow on a tree or rooftop. There are many ways to expand your awareness of the many riches of God's creation through the literature and arts of diverse cultures and systems of thought. The following covenants address this arena:

- I promise to regularly read classics as well as contemporary theology and literature.

- I promise to explore a culture or nation with which I am unfamiliar either through reading or dialoguing with members of that culture.

- I promise to respond to new ideas with openness before analyzing them.

- I promise to fully embrace God's affirmation that I am created in God's image and am worthy of love.

FOUR

TRANSFORMING SPIRIT

Ministry is a multidimensional profession. Vital and creative pastors must weave together the ancient traditions and contemporary responsibilities of their calling as they imagine the emergent future of the church, nation, and planet. In the course of a week, pastors may be called to be rabbis and teachers, evangelists and motivational speakers, administrators and building managers, counselors and spiritual guides, and prophets and advocates. Many pastors struggle to find a dynamic and lively spiritual center around which to integrate their many and diverse callings in ministry.

Steve notes wistfully that "before seminary I had a lively prayer life. During seminary I attended chapel regularly and took classes in spirituality, but now that I'm in the pastorate, I barely get a chance to pray or meditate. I need to find a time and a practice that fits my schedule and responsibilities as a pastor, spouse, and parent." Judith strives for integrity, but finds herself "totally fragmented" whenever she has to balance her ordinary ministerial tasks with an unexpected funeral or scheduled Saturday wedding.

John notes that "there is a painful disconnect between my prayer life and pastoral vocation and administrative duties. Theologically, I believe that God is present in everyone's life and that God will provide for what we really need, but as soon as there is conflict in the congregational session meeting or the trustees bring up money issues, I lose my sense of God's providential care. Like the disciples during the storm at sea, all I see is the threat. And, on a hard day, I forget that my secretary needs my patience and care as much as my critical comments." Emily confesses that, despite the external successes of her ministry, "I am good at doing, but lousy with being. As long as I am starting a new project, serving on a task force, traveling to a denominational meeting, or leading worship or preaching, my life seems complete. But, the minute I stop to pray or attempt to meditate, I feel like a failure. I just can't slow down. I know I need to, because I feel like I am accomplishing a lot on the outside, but becoming more harried and superficial on the inside. My lack of prayer time is even effecting my preaching." These three, like many other pastors, need to feed the fires of the spirit within in order to illuminate and inspire vital spirituality and social engagement in their congregations.

While there is no one definition of spirituality, we have stated before that we believe that healthy pastoral spirituality involves a sense of God's presence and guidance that integrates and illuminates the whole of a person's personal, professional, and relational life at the micro and macro levels. In the midst of the living dynamics of creative and transformative ministry, a commitment to spiritual practices and spiritual growth enables us to glimpse the deeper and fuller dimensions of our lives and the lives of those with whom we pastor. Only then are we liberated from the clamoring of the false, ego-centered self, so that we may hear God's voice within our own voice and the voices of others and experience God's dynamic life-giving presence imparting depth and meaning to the ordinary and unexpected tasks of ministerial life.

We believe that the spiritual formation of ministers is a creative process that dynamically joins vision and practice, theology and contemplation in a quest to integrate the blessing of God's lively unity, beauty, and wisdom amid the gifts of great diversity. If your spiritual commitments and practices reflect, in good measure, your vision of God, humankind, and creation, then it is important not only to share your vision of God, humankind, and creation, but to explore and develop your own unique vision of the same. Undergirding this book is the belief that vital and healthy ministry finds its inspiration in the vision of a lively, active, and immanent God, who is constantly providing us with all the insights, inspiration, and energy we need to fulfill God's vision in our unique and complex callings. God is always more than we can imagine, yet, mysteriously, God is also as near to us as our next breath.

So too, it is important for us to believe that the last word of God's saving grace has not been spoken! We rejoice that the United Church of Christ, with which we are affiliated, not only proclaims that "God is still speaking" but lifts up a large "comma" as the central symbol for our denomination's open-ended theology and its recent campaign for growth and vitality. The large black comma on a red background is meant to portray the theological point first made, apparently, by entertainer Gracie Allen who once said, "Never put a period where God put a comma!" These words depict a certain liveliness and openness in the divine-human partnership in which God is constantly luring us toward new possibilities for the abundant life God imagines for not only ourselves and our families, but our congregations and the world!

What are the implications of believing that God is continually doing a new thing in each moment of our experience? It means trusting the initiative of God's presence to weave together the many factors of our lives and responsibilities to create a beautiful tapestry of ministerial service and wholeness. At the heart of the spiritual adventures offered to today's pastors by the vision of a lively and immanent God are the twin affirmations: "God is still speaking *to* me." and " God is still speaking *through* me and calling me to share my experience of God's presence with others." How exactly do we do this? We have found that a five-step spiritual process helps us along. If God's transforming spirit is the source, inspiration, and energy that gives meaning and integrity to our lives, then our job is simply to *pause and notice God's presence* and then *open and yield ourselves to it* through specific behavioral responses of stretching and reaching out to others and to God.

A dynamically transforming spirituality calls us to be wise pastors and leaders as well as wise teachers and friends. The biblical Wisdom tradition provides us ample guidance for this enterprise within the theological trajectory embodied within what is known as Wisdom literature. Kate first began to study this tradition and its implications for ministry as part of her doctor of ministry project in the 1970s. Wisdom (Sophia) is "a significant figure for both biblical Judaism and [b]iblical Christianity."[1] Divine Wisdom elicits from her followers a sense of awe and reverence. She helps mediate truth and justice amidst a variety of everyday experiences (Proverbs) as well as the delights and the challenges of creative divine-human partnerships relating not only to nature but also to the cosmos, as described in the books of Ben Sirach, Baruch, and the Wisdom of Solomon in the Hebrew scriptures. The influence of the wisdom tradition is found in Jesus' parables, Paul's epistles, and the letter of James. So too, John's gospel identifies wisdom—Sophia—with the word made flesh (Logos).

Wisdom's poetic, invitational style sagely guides pastors to be attentive to God's presence in both the large and small events of congregational and personal life and to speak the truth in love, pursue the good, and seek justice and righteousness for all. Wisdom calls to pastors not only at the crossroads of their congregational and community activities, but also through the activities of the home and hearth and the beauty and order of nature.

Wisdom invites us to learn to see God in all things and all things in God and give God "awe-full" reverence and honor in all things. Wisdom also calls us to trust God's beneficent presence amidst the encounters of life. This means that as we prepare for a sermon, engage in community organizing to combat violence and racism, lead strategic planning for our congregation, or prepare to visit a grieving family, we are called to pause, notice, open, yield, and respond to God's quiet but persistent presence that connects and integrates the many apparently disparate moments of our lives. Wisdom always seeks to broaden our sense of the spectrum of possibilities. Pastors who listen for and trust Wisdom's call will experience vitality, perspective, patience, and creativity for the long haul and will have the energy to respond to the moment-by-moment cries of creation in their congregations and in the world.

TRANSFORMING WISDOM

In their quest for excellence in ministry, today's pastors may be surprised to discover that more than two thousand years ago, the voice of divine Wisdom (Sophia) provided guidance and inspiration for those, like we, who sought to "think globally and act locally." As you reflect on the spiritual wisdom of Proverbs 8 and Romans 8 we trust that you will find the inspiration and guidance appropriate to your personality type, life experiences, and congregational setting and true help for ministering with vitality, integrity, imagination, and wholeness.

Listen prayerfully to divine Wisdom embodied in these passages. Take a moment to reflect on your own experience of God's wisdom in the ordinary as well as extraordinary moments of your ministry.

> God created me [Wisdom] at the beginning of God's work. . . . I was beside God like a master worker (artist), and I was daily God's delight, rejoicing before God always, rejoicing in God's inhabited world and delighting in the human race. (Prov. 8:22, 30–31)

Wisdom calls us to experience the world as a place of beauty and delight. Those who listen to divine Wisdom experience wonder and joy at the beauty of God in creation and in all of humankind and they seek to share that beauty and joy with others because they know that they are always on holy ground. As "artists of the spirit" who share in the wisdom of the divine artist, wise pastors trust Wisdom to creatively transform the images and words of scripture and their religious traditions so that they are relevant and lively and bring healing and wholeness to their contemporary situation. We awaken to God's holy wisdom in our lives and ministry so that all persons

> may know wisdom and instruction, understanding words of insight, receive instruction in wise dealing, righteousness, justice and equity; that prudence may be given to the simple, knowledge and discretion to the youth—The wise [one] also may hear and increase in learning, and the [person] of understanding acquire skill to understand a proverb and a figure, the words of the wise and their riddles. Awe and reverence for God are the beginning of knowledge; fools despise wisdom and instruction. (Prov. 1:2–7)[2]

Within the communal arena divine Wisdom concerns itself primarily with issues of righteousness, justice, and equity. It is especially concerned with the welfare of the young and the "simple."

The message of Romans 8 goes even further to place our ministerial and congregational calling in the broadest perspective, the interplay of the personal, congregational, and global. Paul's vision of the human and planetary adventure is breathtaking in its integration of every sphere of life in Romans 8:19, 22–23:

> Creation waits with eager longing for the revealing of the children
> of God. . . . We know that the whole creation has been groaning in
> labor pains until now; and not only the creation, but we ourselves,
> who have the first fruits of the Spirit, groan inwardly while we wait
> for our adoption, the redemption of our bodies.

Wisdom's way includes a vision of human suffering—our suffering—as a natural part of the labor pains of all creation seeking the realm of God's shalom—healing and wholeness, justice and peace—for all.

Wisdom reminds us that our well-being, the well-being of others, and, indeed, of all creation itself are intimately connected in a dynamic ecology of grace. Our own spiritual awareness is essential to the fulfillment of planetary life. God's voice moves through broken and unfinished creation and through our own spiritual brokenness and incompleteness seeking wholeness for all. Wisdom's spirit, manifest in Jesus, calls us to say "yes" to our role as God's companions in healing the earth. The cry of creation reminds us that we are embedded in creation, and creation is embedded in us. We live and move and have our being in an interdependent world. In this age of global warming and the rapidly increasing extinction of many species of flora and fauna, wisdom calls us to a certain ecological consciousness in all we do and say as pastors. God's vision for congregations and their spiritual leaders is of one piece with God's call in the nonhuman world.

The relational and communal nature of salvation is never more obvious than in a pastor's vocational life. Illness or conflict in our selves or our family always shapes the life of the church. Conversely, our spiritual stature enlivens and brings wholeness to the congregations we are called to lead. But, more than that, our spirituality has global implications. We cannot find healing apart from the healing of the earth, nor can the earth find healing apart from a creative spirituality of attentive and responsive stewardship. What would it be like for you to really embrace the truth that your health, and prayers, as well as your actions, radiate across the planet, creating life-supporting fields of force and opportunities for personal and global transformation?

Accordingly, spiritual vitality among pastors is more a matter of opening to experiencing God's presence than achieving fixed and inflexible doctrinal clarity. At the same time that we lift up the importance of articulating a clear theological vision for the vitality and health of your ministry, Wisdom also calls us to humbly confess that our experiences and descriptions of God are always finite, fallible, and subject to change as the light of wisdom continues to illumine our lives.

Theological humility means, for instance, that the *kataphatic* vision of "God in all things and all things in God," which inspires our work in this book, is best balanced by recognizing the *apophatic* vision of God's mystery in which no image, even our most articulate visions of God, can encompass the God whose wisdom has created billions of galaxies over thirteen to fifteen billion years.

As you chart your ministerial adventures, Wisdom teaches you to humbly confess the ever present interplay between affirmation and negation, between clarity and mystery that Paul describes in Romans 8:

> Likewise the Spirit helps us in our weakness; for we do not know how to pray as we ought, but that very Spirit intercedes for us with sighs too deep for words. . . . the Spirit intercedes for the saints according to the will of God. (Rom. 8:26, 27b)

Spiritual growth is a creative process that is always venturing into the unknown, guided by the faith that God continues to speak in prophetic utterances calling for peace and justice as well as in gentle "sighs too deep for words," within the movements of your unconscious as well as conscious experience and the almost imperceptible groans of the nonhuman world. Woven into every moment's experience is Wisdom's voice, luring you toward God's vision for the present intimate moment, the world around you, and God's emerging, but uncertain, future. Wisdom's way calls through the cries of creation. Only as you honor and respond to Wisdom's voice in creation will you experience the shining power of God's abundant life in yourself and in your congregational leadership.

In seeing the world through the eyes of Holy Wisdom, you awaken to God's voice not only in the "least of these" in your community, but in the most challenging persons and situations in your congregation. Guided by God's wisdom, embodied in your growing awareness of the "sighs too deep for words" in yourself and those with whom you pastor, you will increasingly be able discern God's unique calling in every moment and relationship. As you learn to discern God's wisdom in your daily life, you will shine forth with energy and power even in challenging times. Sustained by your connection with God, abundant life will be a reality for you, burnout a virtual impossibility!

THE FIVE-FOLD PATH OF PASTORAL SPIRITUALITY

Over the years, we both have been inspired personally and professionally by the Shalem Institute for Spiritual Formation and the insightful reflections of one of the its founders, Gerald May, on the spiritual lives of spiritual leaders.[3] May sees spiritual formation and growth as involving the following practices: *pausing, noticing, opening,* and *yielding and stretching.* In the interplay of contemplation, study, and action, essential to transforming ministry, we add a fifth practice, the practice of *reaching out and responding* with what we have experienced in the interplay of opening to God and yielding to God's vision for this unique moment and encounter.

One translation of Psalm 46 invites the reader to "pause awhile and know that I am God." The art of pausing amid the busyness of vocational and family obligations transforms our experience of time and relationships. Many pastors note that their most important ministry occurs in synchronous moments when they slow down and pause for a conversation over coffee, gaze out their study window at the lively play of children in the church playground, sit down to rest with a spouse or partner, or take time to truly listen to the church secretary share about her child's recent marriage. Theological vision is found in the pausing as well as acting. In pausing, we slow down our perception of the flow of time so that we can truly awaken to the God-moments and synchronous occurrences that come to us every day.

Pastors would greatly benefit from gently reviving the practice of "praying the hours" throughout the day by pausing to breathe in and out as they say a brief prayer of gratitude, petition, intercession, or adoration. A commitment to pausing before God throughout the day transformed Diane's ministry. "I used to race from one appointment to another throughout the day. After supper, I would hit the computer for another few hours to answer mail and work on projects. My head was whirling so much that I had to take a drink or sleeping pill to get to sleep." As she took a hard look at her life, Diane realized that living on the surface, even for the sake of doing God's work, was not only robbing her of peace of mind, but trivializing her relationship with God and those she sought to serve. "I realized that God doesn't want my superficiality, God wants my undivided attention. God wants me to go deeper, trusting God alone in all my relationships. I realized that serving God meant doing only one thing at a time and ministering to only one person at a time, even when I preached to a full congregation on Sunday morning. I had to trust God to complete what I left unfinished." Diane committed herself to the simple practice of pausing throughout her busy day to breathe in God's spacious presence. "Throughout the day, whenever I move from one task to another, I close my eyes for a moment and take three deep and holy breaths. Even if I'm going down the hallway to the prayer shawl group or to consult with the custodian, I pause to breathe."

Diane has made one other adjustment in her practice of ministry. She has chosen to end the day not at her computer, arranging details for the next day's meetings or working on sermons or reports, but in her easy chair, reading poetry and fiction, listening to music, or talking with a friend. "I work hard, but when I relax during the last few hours of the day, I go to sleep the minute after I say my evening prayers." In pausing for God's presence throughout the day, Diane embodies the faith she intellectually affirms—the belief that God is present in her life and that divine providence guides the affairs of persons and institutions.

When we take time to practice pausing in the course of the day, we soon begin to *notice* the Spirit's revealing presence everywhere. Ordinary encounters become synchronous opportunities and, at times, even theophanies as we begin to see "God in all things and all things in God."

A plaque on our fireplace mantle bears the words of an Elizabeth Barrett Browning poem.

> *. . . Earth's crammed with heaven*
> *and every common bush afire with God;*
> *And only he who sees, takes off his shoes,*
> *The rest sit round it and pluck blackberries. . .* [4]

While we both delight in the taste of fresh, organic blackberries, we recognize that our holistic spiritual journey invites us to see holiness in everyday things, even eating blackberries and marveling at the complexity of bushes from which they burst forth. The truth is that Annie Dillard's "tree with lights" is hiding within every tree and bush. So, too, the face of God shines through every congregant when we take the time to pause and notice each person's beauty prayerfully and with reverence.

When we pause and notice, we discover that the world is much "more" than we can imagine. The ever-present God energizes all things, consecrates each task, and inspires each encounter. When David began to "notice" the movement of God's Spirit, anonymously moving throughout the events of his day, he felt "born again" for vital ministry. "After fifteen years of congregational ministry, and ten in the same congregation, I felt like I had 'been there, done that,' as I looked at the current state of my life and ministry. I was losing my edge and sense of adventure. Even family life had also become routine." After attending a day retreat with Oasis Ministries for Spiritual Formation in Pennsylvania, David reawakened to the hidden riches of everyday ministry. "As I spent time in silent prayer, I asked the question, 'how can I regain my sense of vocational energy?' While I didn't receive a dramatic revelation, I felt a divine nudge, telling me, 'the energy is already there. Look around and you will see.'"[5] Now, David delights in the ordinary tasks of ministry and home life. Whenever he begins to feel stressed and dull, he returns to his circle of silence, whether in the church's sanctuary or walking in the neighborhood surrounded church.

When we pause and notice the wonder of life, we awaken to the fiery, bright hues of Pentecost and the shining gifts of Epiphany year round. We come alive, prepared to see God in all things and share God with all persons.

In the healing of a hearing impaired man, Jesus places his hands on his ears and cries out "be opened."[6] Once oblivious to the sounds of creation, now he can hear the wondrous symphony of life in all its many voices. *Opening* to God and life itself can be one of the greatest challenges in the spiritual journey of ministers. Too often, out of fear, trauma, fatigue, habit, or choice, we close ourselves off experientially, intellectually, physically, relationally, and energetically to the wondrous energy of life. We need the "celestial surgeon" to pierce the armor that we have erected against our own pain and the pain of the world.[7] This holy opening can take place in many ways—through an encounter with a spiritual friend, spiritual director, or therapist who prayerfully mirrors our pain and hope; through a silent retreat where stillness awakens us to the voice of God in our many voices; through the "dark night" of sickness of body, mind, or spirit, that breaks down our barriers and invites us to trust God alone for our deliverance; through healing touch that opens us to new holy energies and sooths previous wounds of the spirit; or through honest self-searching of feelings and memories in the context of psychotherapy.

Opening to God and to life itself in its fullness is an act of hope and trust. As one pastor notes, "I never knew how closed off I was to God's love until I was hospitalized following back surgery. Then, I discovered the meaning of grace—in allowing myself to accept the kindness of friends and strangers; in accepting my vulnerability and dependence; and then reclaiming the power of the healing God that flows through me to others."

While we are seldom ever fully open to reality, pausing and noticing enables us to grow in stature and trust. In opening to the universe [of life] within us and beyond us, we can say "yes" to God's "signs and wonders" in all their varied complexity, joy, and sorrow. We can catch a glimpse of our destiny as "great souled" persons, living in the spirit of Jesus.

Donna seeks to be open to God in all the encounters of life and ministry. "I realized that I had to change my whole approach to life in order to be open to God's voice in creation. I had to totally let go of my tightly held agenda. While I planned my days and weeks in advance, I had to be willing to stop on a dime if God called me through an auto accident, an angry parishioner, a questioning teen, or a trauma survivor. I also had to be willing to stop on a dime if my daughter was feeling insecure after a hard day at school or my husband upset by the challenges of his job." To her surprise, Donna has discovered that she has to "plan to be open in order to *be open,*" even if all her plans are provisional and are subject to change on a moment's notice. "Pray and plan is my new motto." Donna states. "I pray to be open to God as I plan each day, and I plan prayerfully to balance my agenda with the surprises that God will place on my pathway." Authentic openness is grounded in intentionality, and not control. In "planning to be open" to God's call through the events of our lives, we also honor God's call to be faithful and professional in the tasks of ministry. As Donna admits, "I always have a plan, but now I trust God's wisdom enough to recognize that God's plans are bigger and better than my own. Whenever I let go of my small plans, God fills my spirit with a more exciting plan and the energy and time to attempt it!"

The balance of radical openness and tightly scheduled ministry is challenging, but Jesus is our guide in this process. Although he was always available to respond to the unexpected needs of others, Jesus was clearly guided by a vision that embraced novelty and order as essential to his calling as God's teacher, healer, and savior. Openness enables us to embrace the sorrow of the world as well as the divine resources for healing and wholeness flowing through our lives. As we open to these divine resources in the midst of our schedules, we are energized rather than depleted by the challenges of ministry.

Many mainstream and progressive Christians have difficulty affirming the role of *yielding* as an essential step in spiritual transformation. To many of us, yielding implies passivity, patriarchy, and subservience to power. In contrast, we believe that our role as partners in God's healing of the world and our congregations suggests action and responsibility rather than passive obedience. Despite our own problems with using the word "yielding," we believe the word points to the deeper reality of loosening and stretching out in order to align ourselves with God's vision for our lives, our congregations, and the planet. From this perspective, yielding involves a commitment to listen for God's voice as we seek to articulate our own vision of our lives and ministries. As Gerald May notes, when we yield to God's presence in our lives, we must *stretch* in order to claim God's new life that beckons us.

Gerald May contrasts "willfulness" with "willingness" in his understanding of yielding as a spiritual practice. Willfulness focuses on the ego and its narrow interests. Willfulness exaggerates our autonomy, individuality, and isolation. Emphasizing autonomy, we neglect the cries of creation and God's wisdom for our lives. Autonomous, ego-centered leadership focuses on our vision of ministry and fails to notice God's wisdom working within the voices and gifts of our congregation. Ego-centered leadership involves winning theological, ecclesiastical, and administrative battles rather than discerning God's Spirit moving in our midst. Willful ministry separates clergy and laity, us and them, and friend and foe.

In contrast, spiritual leadership, guided by willingness, recognizes that "we do not know how to pray as we ought" (Rom. 8:26). Willingness is the art of embracing the reality of vulnerable and mutual interdependence by which we listen for God's voice in the many voices of life. The small, ego-centered, and defensive self gives way to the "greater self," reflecting God within us. The willing self is never alone, nor is it without resources. God will provide abundant life to those who embrace the dynamic interdependence of life. As one pastor notes, "When I let go of my need to be right and listen to God's vision for my life, I am no longer defensive or afraid. I trust that God will give me the wisdom I need to lead this congregation faithfully. Even when there's conflict, I know that God will show me a way to help this congregation find its way." For the willing spirit, there is no *other*; my well-being and success are interconnected with yours, and opponents can be embraced as the source of new ideas. The willing spirit rejoices in God's abundant life coursing through her or his own ministry and the ministries of laypersons within her or his congregation.

When we yield to God's voice in creation, our vision stretches and expands and our lives gain integrity. The wisdom of pausing, noticing, opening, yielding, and stretching is that we discover that we are really doing just *one* thing in ministry, seeking to discern and follow God's guidance in every situation. We move from fragmentation to unity of spirit, as we allow God to knit together the many tasks of ministry. Although we continue to recognize our personal fallibility and limited perspective, we courageously share the truth we have found whether in the pulpit, classroom, church board, or local political arena.

All life is a call and response. When we yield, stretch, and shape our lives around God's call, we find the inspiration, creativity, and energy to claim our responsibility as God's active partners in transforming the world and our congregations. Liberated from the need to succeed or have our own way, we can trust that God is doing a good work in our lives and congregations even when it cannot yet be discerned or when we must let of our plans in order to awaken to God's vision working in surprising ways in the insights of laypersons within our congregation.

We believe that God's call in our lives and the world provides both the vision of shalom and the energy to respond to this vision in our unique way. Implied by this dynamic interplay of call and response is the insight that faithful responsiveness involves a certain amount of improvisation. God wants us to "color outside the lines" as we claim our role as artists of our own lives and congregations. The God who delighted in the works of dancing and creative wisdom delights in our own creativity. While our responses will always be imperfect and shaped by our own limitations, God will continually provide new visions for faithfulness as our lives and ministries unfold. As more than one pastor in Lancaster Theological Seminary's ministerial excellence programs has noted, "Once I let go of my own self-centered vision and opened to God's dream for my life and congregation, I became free to create in new and surprising ways. I don't know what will happen next. But I do know that God will supply my needs and that God will place the persons and resources in my life that will help me be faithful in my calling."

Called to be partners with divine wisdom, we can do greater things than we can imagine. We can trust God's dream as we seek to be lively change agents in our congregations and in the world. When we realize that the whole energy of God's universe is flowing through us, the same demands that lead some pastors to experience burnout can become our raw materials for creative personal and professional transformation.

FEEDING THE MINISTERIAL FIRE

Spiritual formation in ministry involves seeing "God in all things and all things in God." For those with eyes to see, there is a "burning bush" around every corner. The gift of experiencing the world through the lens of God's wisdom enables each of us to discover and manifest God's presence in every act of ministry.

A Holistic Spiritual Practice

In this practice, we invite you as you go through your day to take a moment whenever you begin a task to notice more fully what is going on around or in yourself. Pause and take a deep breath and ask to experience the situation or person from God's perspective. Open yourself to what you experience as you breathe your prayer for God's wisdom as you begin each task, whether answering the phone, checking e-mail, or meeting with your secretary. At the conclusion of each, take time to breathe deeply and give thanks for God's presence and guidance in that particular task.

A Practice for Healthy Ministry

Healing and wholeness are a matter of holy awareness. Many pastors are so busy about their ministerial responsibilities that they pay virtually no attention to their physical and spiritual health and well-being. In so doing, they miss out on one of God's primary vehicles of revelation, God's word made flesh in the life of Jesus and in our own mortal flesh.

In the following spiritual practice, we invite you simply to take notice of your current physical and spiritual well-being at least twice each day. Take a moment to breathe deeply, gently becoming aware of the simple joy of inhaling and exhaling.

Pause as you breathe in order to receive God's graceful wisdom with every breath.

Notice your current state of wellness. Do you feel any stress? Are you at home in your flesh? If you are anxious, what is the source? Take time to breathe through any stress, anxiety, or pain.

Open to the totality of your experience, including the energy of God flowing in and out of your life with each breath. This energy flows through your whole being.

Yield and stretch to God's movements in your body and your intellectual and emotional life. Listen for God's unique movements within your organs, respiration, immune system, digestive system, and reproductive system. Yield to God's moments within your flesh and blood, and body and spirit. Listen to divine insight flowing into your mind and spirit. As a symbol of your commitment to stretching in response to God's vision, you might get up from your desk and do a few gentle physical stretches, raising your hands toward the heavens.

Respond. In this "wholly" or "holy" reading of your body, mind, and spirit, listen for God's call within your whole being. What is divine Wisdom saying to you in terms of your wholeness? In what way will you respond to God's call in your life? Where is God calling you as a transforming leader?

An Affirmation of Faith

The five-fold path of spiritual transformation is a matter of intentionality and practice, related to every aspect of life from greeting newcomers in the narthex to playing ultimate Frisbee with the youth group. In the spirit of the wisdom of Brother Lawrence and Gerald May, we can practice God's presence in every moment through choosing to *pause, notice, open, yield,* and *respond,* regardless of the time and place. When we listen to Wisdom's call, we experience God in all things, and all things in God. The following affirmations awaken us to God's ongoing revelation in our lives.

- I see God in all things and all things in God.

- I practice the presence of God in every situation and encounter.

- I pause, notice, open, yield, and respond to God's presence in every situation and encounter.

A Covenant of Wholeness and Vitality in Ministry

Mindfulness is one of the most essential, but also most difficult, disciplines of transformative and vital ministry. Self-awareness in ministry is not ultimately one more thing to do, but rather the way we experience our lives and ministry. In this chapter, we invite you to covenant regularly to *pause, notice, open, yield,* and *respond* to God in a particular aspect of your life. Awareness is realized one moment and one task at a time. In this spirit, you may choose the following covenant:

- I covenant to become aware of God's presence in congregational board meetings.

- I covenant to pause, notice, open, yield, and respond to God in my family life and committed relationships.

- I covenant to practice God's presence as I go from task to task in ministry.

FIVE

TRANSFORMING TIME

Recently, when we were program leaders for a United Church of Christ Summer Conference at Star Island, New Hampshire, we observed a number of tee-shirts that read "I'm on island time." Eight miles off the coast of New Hampshire, we were far from calendars, deadlines, and meetings. For a week, we enjoyed the world of an upper-class nineteenth-century hotel, which had not been significantly updated for this century. Although there was electricity and cold running water in our cottage, we had to adjust to life without high speed internet service or cable television, as well as spotty cell phone reception, and hot "public" showers twice a week. While the week was filled with activities, in many ways time slowed down for everyone on the island. The days began with the pink rays of the rising sun and ended before 10:00 P.M. Time was full and spacious, as spacious as the star-filled skies and rolling waves, far from the bright lights of Portsmouth.[1]

Contrast this experience with the confession of a pastor in his second year of ministry, "I wake up anxious each morning. When I think of the never-ending tasks at church, my heart races. Then, when I ponder my responsibilities as a parent and spouse, I panic because there just aren't enough hours in the day or days in the week to balance the church and family life. I'm doing the best I can to juggle everything, but I feel like I'm always letting somebody down." Despite his excellence in ministry, this "effective" young pastor is already in brown-out and may soon descend into burnout, a professional malaise characterized by the contrasting experiences of panic, lethargy, anger, and hopelessness.

Physicists remind us that both time and space are relative, rather than uniform, in nature. Time and space are dependent on the interrelatedness of events—where we stand and how we look at the world—rather than the evenly moving hands of the clock. Long before the advent of contemporary physics, the biblical tradition recognized the dynamic and relational nature of time, distinguishing *chronos* time, or evenly flowing and predictable times of the seasons and days, from *kairos* time, the unique moments of divine fullness and revelation that turn time and space upside down—moments of divine healing, transformation, and resurrection. While the time of our lives appears to pass quickly from birth to death, punctuated by "deadlines" and discrete events, there are deeper threads of time within the passing of our lives. God's lively time flows infinitely and deeply as it embraces all things intimately in God's evolving and everlasting life.

Physicians, such as Larry Dossey, have noted the growing contemporary reality of "time sickness" or "hurry sickness." Where once "time saving" advances were expected to lead us toward more leisurely living, the opposite has occurred: the Internet and cell phones have cluttered and interrupted our time menacingly. Our attitudes toward time are a factor in overall well-being. Some days, we are not only busy with many tasks, we also feel busy—we have that sense of pressure that is physiological as well as mental and emotional. On such days, which can become weeks, our perception of time is one of stress and distress, rather than spaciousness and peace.

As you look at your calendars or scribble in your personal digital assistants (PDAs), are you overwhelmed by the time demands of congregational and judicatory meetings, annual reports, sermon preparation, hospital visitation, and pastoral care appointments? Do activities that are intended to be joyful and sustaining in ministry, such as sermon and worship preparation, become tasks rather than opportunities to deepen our faith? During pastoral care appointments, do you stifle yawns and glance at your study clock, already preparing for your next appointment?

Do you know what we mean? Take a few minutes and look at your weekly schedule. How do you feel as you consider the tasks that lie before you this week? How can you fit times of reflection and prayer into your schedule? Take another moment and consider how it feels to be busy. Then take a few deep breaths or visualize a place of quiet beauty and remember what it's like to be at peace.

TIME AND REFRESHMENT

Jesus practiced a healthy approach to time and vocation in his role as his disciples' mentor, teacher, and spiritual guide. As we noted earlier, after sending his disciples out on their first solo mission as teachers and healers (Mark 6:7–13, 30–32), Jesus invites them to go on a retreat with him. Near burnout, Jesus' disciples needed a time to pause in God's presence:

> He said to them, "Come away to a deserted place all by yourselves and rest awhile." For many were coming and going, and they had no leisure even to eat. (Mark 6:30)

Recently, Bruce read this story as part of a *lectio divina* exercise with a group of new pastors participating in Lancaster Theological Seminary's Wholeness in Ministry program. They especially resonated with the sentence: "For many were coming and going, and they had no leisure even to eat." One pastor noted that most of her eating was "drive by" in nature—a fast food hamburger or sandwich on the way to a hospital call. Another described eating at his desk, humorously painting the picture of the phone in one hand, sandwich in the other, the cell phone going off, and eyes fixed on the most recent e-mail—all at the same time. In reflecting on the passage, another pastor exclaimed, "that's my spiritual life. The minute I close my eyes to pray, the phone rings. I have to make a choice. Will I answer the phone or rest a few minutes in God's presence? I know the minute I answer the phone, my prayer time will end." One pastor chimed in, "thank God for voice mail and caller ID. I used to answer every phone call, even at home and at the dinner table. Now, I know I can take an extra minute for prayer or study or time with my daughter, knowing I can always return the call in ten minutes."

Compassionate, vital, renewed, and renewing ministry is the gift of God's abundant life. We can transform time through contemplation, recreation, rest, and intentional rotation of ministerial activities from analytic to artistic and business to study. Instead of running on empty, pastors can run "on plenty," as Suzanne Schmidt and Krista Kurth affirm, by committing themselves to following a healthy rhythm of action and rest.[2]

When we do not take adequate time for rest and contemplation, for simple replenishment by whatever means work best for us, we become distracted, impatient, weary, and stale. This is one of the messages of the gospel narrative of Mary and Martha. Jesus' response to Martha is not motivated by her focus on preparing the meal rather than entering into conversation, but her attitude toward the task at hand. "Anxious about many things," Martha becomes angry at her more contemplative sister Mary. Her anxiety leads to alienation as she forgets the deeper meaning of hospitality. Martha needs to take time for laughter and conversation, theological reflection and relaxation. Caught up in the tension of her tasks, Martha has lost the spirit of the moment. Given her more task-oriented personality, simply sitting while food needed to be prepared might have been too difficult for Martha. But, rather than critiquing her sister for her attentiveness to Jesus, what if Martha might have suggested that the two of them take an after-dinner walk while Mary did the dishes? Could it have been that Martha's time consciousness got in the way of her experiencing God's everlasting now? Perhaps, had she breathed deeply and prayed her preparation, Martha might have maintained a spirit of calm and equanimity that would have enabled her to participate in the conversation even as she was preparing supper.

Times of rest, whether we are meditating, walking our prayers, dancing, knitting a prayer shawl, chanting the "Jesus prayer," or praying for loved ones as we prepare a meal, awaken us to God's spacious everlasting now. In contrast to Martha's experience, one busy pastor takes time to visualize and pray for those who will gather around the dinner table when she prepares meals for her family or a dish for the church potluck. "Although my husband and I share household responsibilities, I often come home from a busy day emotionally unprepared to cook dinner. While I sometimes call out for pizza or Chinese food, I have also come to relish cooking simple meals in a prayerful way. As I cut vegetables, prepare salad, or add sauce to the pasta, I visualize and thank God for each member of my family. I used to see preparing a dish for the potluck as an inconvenience and source of irritation. But, now, when I have time to prepare a dessert or salad, I visualize the social hall and see the smiling, happy faces of those who will gather for fellowship and prayer." Another pastor experiences peace while he edits the church newsletter by "taking a moment to remind myself that these administrative tasks reflect my sense of calling, love of my family, and commitment to our congregation's mission."

Our experience of time can bring us joy or anxiety. How we experience time is partly a matter or attitude or choice. Perspective changes everything. Recently, Bruce reflected on the use of the word "deadline" to describe the date when a project should be done. It is unfortunate that "deadlines" connect time with punishment and death rather than adventure and opportunity. Although there may be consequences for work that is not finished at the appropriate time, Bruce now uses the term "lifeline" to describe the duration of tasks. "Lifelines" define our work as an opportunity for vitality, growth, novelty, and joy, despite the inherent limitations of our time schedules. Lifelines are about positive goals and the fulfillment of values and dreams. God's time is always full even as it unfolds one moment at a time in partnership with the emerging universe and our daily tasks.

TIME AND SELF-DIFFERENTIATION

Getting a "view from the balcony" is essential to healthy, vital, and transformative leadership, according to Harvard professor Ronald Heifitz. Pastoral leadership is a matter of perspective, of seeing the world through the eyes of what Craig Dykstra calls the "pastoral imagination," the ability to integrate theology, spirituality, and ministerial practice. Accordingly, healthy pastors see their spiritual leadership as a marathon and not a sprint. Vital and effective pastoral leadership takes time in order to earn trust, understand the congregation, make informed healthy decisions, and prayerfully and creatively respond to conflict. Pastoral wisdom includes the gift of transforming time in such a way that long-term visions can be kept in sight and mindfully embodied in everyday decisions.

Healthy and vital pastoral leadership requires creative self-differentiation that preserves one's integrity and vision while also maintaining healthy concern and interdependence. Earlier in this book, we described the interplay of Jesus' prayer time and the demands of his disciples, described in Mark 1, in terms of self-care and ministerial vision. This same passage also highlights Jesus' practice of visionary and self-differentiated leadership. According to the Gospel of Mark, Jesus goes to a quiet place for prayer and meditation following a day filled with teaching, healing, preaching, and socializing. Listen once again to this description of Jesus' commitment to joining vision, contemplation, and vocation.

> In the morning, while it was still very dark, he got up and went out to a deserted place, and there he prayed. And Simon and his companions hunted for him. When they found him, they said to him, "Everyone is searching for you." He answered, "Let us go to the neighboring towns, so that I may proclaim the message there also; for that is what I came out to do." (Mark 1:35–38)

This passage is a gold mine from the perspective of congregational systems theory and its understanding of the role of anxiety, triangulation, and self-differentiation in the life of communities. When Jesus retreats to the wilderness in order to align himself with God's vision for his life and replenish his spirit, his disciples go in search of him. In fact, they "hunt" for him anxiously like children whose sense of security depends on their parents' physical presence. In a classic example of triangulation, they assert that "everyone is searching for you," instead of confessing their own anxiety. The disciples, along with certain of the townspeople, would like Jesus to remain in Capernaum as their "resident" chaplain and healer. But their good intentions run counter to Jesus' understanding of God's vocation for his life. Although he does not abandon his friends and students or even challenge their desire for him to settle in Capernaum, Jesus makes clear to them that he is called to wider mission. "Let us go to neighboring towns, so that I may proclaim the message there also; for that is what I came out to do." Calmly and yet decisively, Jesus shares his calling while inviting his disciples to a deeper understanding of God and their respective missions.

As a model of self-differentiated and nonanxious leadership, Jesus reminds us that time-transforming solitude enables us to not only replenish our spirits, but also maintain the integrity of vision and open-heartedness necessary for compassionate and effective ministry. Poorly thought-out decisions, made in the context of fatigue, anxiety, hurry, or congregational pressure, seldom embody God's aim at wholeness for congregational, personal, or professional life. Stepping back from the urgency of the day enables us to gain perspective and discern spiritually sound and administratively effective ways to respond to congregational challenge.

THIS IS THE DAY!

Bruce awakens each morning with two affirmations in his heart and mind, "this is the day that God has made; I will rejoice and be glad in it" and "what great thing will I experience or be asked to do today?" In the biblical tradition, each moment reflects God's wisdom. God's lively intelligence and creativity breathe over the formless void, spin forth galaxies, move within human institutions, and encounter us in dramatic and apparently "ordinary" moments of our lives. "The whole earth is filled God's glory" (Isa. 6:3) and each moment is a holy moment, bringing forth something novel and unrepeatable.

Transforming time involves experiencing God's presence both in the grandeur of the universe and in the ticking of the clock. All things exist in God's "everlasting now" as God's dynamic embrace of the impact of the past is balanced by a robust hope of the future in each emerging present moment.

The biblical tradition captures the vision of God's everlasting life amid the brevity of our lives in the counsel "Teach us to count our days that we may gain a wise heart" (Psa. 90:12). What would it be like for you to honor the fact that, although our lives flow quickly from birth to death, each moment of your life is of everlasting consequence? As the philosopher Alfred North Whitehead notes, each moment perishes and yet lives evermore in the divine memory and the ongoing universe.[3] Though dwarfed by the space-time immensity of the universe, our lives can still be a tipping point between life and death in our families, congregations, and in the planetary adventure itself. In the spirit of the panentheistic motto "God in all things, and all things in God" that is central to the theology of this text, we can also affirm, "God is in each moment and each moment is in God."

Transforming time is the gift of living mindfully the hours, days, and months of our lives. Monastic traditions focus on the passing of each day through the practice of "praying the hours." From awakening before dawn to preparing for the evening's rest, the monastic day is defined by prayer.[4] Following the spirit of Paul's counsel to the Thessalonians, monks and spirit persons of all centuries are called to "rejoice always, pray without ceasing, give thanks in all circumstances; for this is the will of God in Christ Jesus for you" (1 Thess. 5:16–18). One pastor embodies a contemporary version of the "divine office" or "praying the hours" in the context of his very active personal and professional schedule. "After I wake up, I take a few minutes for morning prayer, using the Episcopal Book of Common Prayer; after breakfast I read scripture in the spirit of *lectio divina*; before lunch I take time for a few minutes of prayerful silence; as I leave for home, whether at church or on a pastoral call, I pause awhile to open to God's presence in my vocation as a husband and father; and before retiring, I go outside and gaze at the heavens, taking time for prayers of thanksgiving for the day passed and petition for the hours of sleep and the new day to which I will awaken."

Paul's counsel is not just for monks; it can be embodied by busy pastors, lay leaders, and professors alike. Prayer weaves together the time of lives. Our own spiritual path as pastors has been inspired by the wisdom of Celtic Christianity. We invite today's pastors to explore "living a Celtic day" as one way of experiencing God's fullness in the ordinary and surprising tasks of ministry. The Celtic vision of "thin places" as the intersection of time and eternity inspires us to consider "thin times," holy moments revealing God's dynamic inspiration in the passage of time.[5]

The Celtic day begins with prayer. The fabled St. Patrick began his day with the following affirmation:

> *I arise today with the might of heaven;*
> *The rays of the sun, the beams of the moon,*

The glory of fire, the speed of wind,
The depth of sea, the stability of earth, the hardness of rock.[6]

A Celtic homemaker begins her or his day with a prayer for kindling the morning fire: "This morning, as I kindle the fire upon my hearth, I pray that the flame of God's love may burn in my heart, and in the hearts of all I meet today."[7] Later, as the working day begins, a dairy farmer prays her or his daily tasks:

"Bless O God my little cow
Bless O God my desire;
Bless Thou my partnership
And the milking of my hands, O God."[8]

In the midst of his daily journey, a Celtic pilgrim prays, "Bless to me, God, each thing mine eye sees; Bless, to me, God, each thing my ear hears. . . . Each thing I pursue, each lure that tempts my will, the zeal that seeks my living soul, the Three that seek my heart."[9] Day ends, as it began, with a prayer, "I lie down this night with God, and God will lie down with me. I lie down this night with Christ, and Christ will lie down with me. I lie down this night with the Spirit, and the Spirit will lie down with me."[10] No moment is too small or too large for God's care and inspiration.

Our perspective becomes global and our experience of time expands when we make a commitment to praying our days from morning to night. Take a moment to consider your day: What tasks occupy your time? What routine activities characterize each day? How do you respond to these varied tasks, from checking e-mail and writing a sermon to working on the church newsletter or visiting the hospital?

God is truly in the details, shaping each moment of time and calling us to receive grace as we claim our role as God's partners in transforming the world. When we attune ourselves to God's presence in the passing moments of the day, even interruptions can call us to prayerful companionship. We realize that God is inspiring us in every synchronous encounter and scheduled, or unscheduled, meeting.

As we noted earlier, given the unexpected realities of death, illness, and celebration, pastors cannot "manage time," but they can be intentional about responding to the movement of time from moment to moment and day to day. Susan experiences God's presence in her morning cup of coffee as she prays over the appointments she has planned for the day ahead.[11] After a time of devotion, she continues her prayer life as she checks her e-mail, closing her eyes, taking a deep breath, and "praying the seconds" between logging on and receiving the overnight mail. "These are simple things, but they start my day right where it belongs—in God's care."

Greg parks at the farthest end of the parking lot when he makes hospital calls and breathes deeply as he circles the hospital before he makes his first visit. "The five minutes of walking clears my head and opens my heart. In my walk, I leave the drive and events of the day in the car so that I can be fully present in that holy moment with someone who needs my undivided attention and prayerfulness." As he listens to the church chimes, hour by hour throughout the day, Steve stops a moment simply to breathe deeply and ask for divine guidance. "Sometimes I anticipate the chimes," Steve notes, "and stop for a moment each hour to be still in God's presence. My whole day becomes a prayer when I take time to listen for God's voice in the chiming bells."

Prayerful days invite us to prayerful weeks. The rhythm of preaching can be a call to prayer throughout the week. Each Monday, Patricia, along with thousands of pastors, consults the lectionary for the next Sunday's readings. She gently bathes herself in the scriptures, letting the words flow into her mind and heart meditatively. Although she eventually consults various commentaries and online resources, Patricia's greatest joy in preaching is the opportunity to live with the scripture and let it bubble up in *lectio divina* style throughout the week. "Where else could I get paid for reading the Bible! Even the tough verses are a gift. They challenge me to go beyond easy answers and embrace new ideas. The Sunday scriptures are my companions throughout the week, the lenses through which I see my life and ministry. I never know on Monday where the scripture will take me. There's always something new in preaching and ministry."

While it is difficult for many pastors and lay persons to experience Sabbath, given the 24/7 nature of ministerial life today, nevertheless, many pastors choose to refresh and revitalize themselves by practicing a spiritual Sabbath every week, typically on some other day than Sunday! Such pastors embody Abraham Joshua Heschel's affirmation that the Sabbath is the "sanctification of time." As Heschel notes, openness to the Sabbath enables us "to be attached to holiness in time, to be attached to sacred events, to learn how to consecrate sanctuaries that emerge from the magnificent stream of the year."[12]

While Jesus occasionally healed on the Sabbath in response to human need, it is clear that he ordinarily practiced Sabbath time and honored the Sabbath traditions of his faith. In like manner, you are challenged to embrace a theology of Sabbath, an affirmation that because God is present in your life, congregation, and the world, you can rest awhile, trusting in God's care for the ultimate realities of your life.

Deborah sees Sabbath as essential to her ministry. "I don't always get a twenty-four-hour Sabbath, especially with two teenage children and a husband; but on Mondays, when my children are at school and my husband at work, I covenant to study and pray in the morning, and spend time with friends over lunch. By four o'clock, when the kids get home, I am once again renewed and refreshed, ready to greet them and go back to the challenges of ministry." Heschel asserts that for those who practice Sabbath, a sense of peace attends their daily lives: "the Sabbath surrounds you wherever you go."[13] Even though you need not be legalistic about your Sabbath time, you can plan for several hours each week to bathe yourself in beauty, great ideas, and divine care. Sabbath time is not a "day off" from work, but a "sanctuary of time," that gives life, direction, and vitality to your ministry and family time. Trusting God with the totality of our lives, we can embody the spirit of John Wesley, "Though I am always in haste, I am never in a hurry because I never undertake more work that I can go through with calmness of spirit."[14]

Sabbath calm gives us the vision to discern what is truly important in our lives and ministry. As we practice Sabbath time, we discover that God, who works while we rest, will bring forth a harvest of righteousness in our lives and ministries when we are awake!

Prayerful days and weeks invite us to live a prayerful year by celebrating the dynamic movement of the seasons of the Christian year. The liturgical seasons provide pastors an annual opportunity to weave together novelty and order, surprise and repetition, in their professional lives. Although each of the seasons repeats the ancient cycle of Advent, Christmas, Epiphany, Lent, Holy Week, Easter, and Pentecost, each season—like the four seasons of the calendar year and the seasons of our personal lives—reveals something new amid the faithful predictability of life.

As we have asserted earlier, we believe that vital ministry is alive and attentive to the interplay of structure and freedom, of order and novelty. The faithful God, whose mercy and love endures forever, is always doing a "new thing" in our lives and in the world. Our calling is to be open and responsive to God's call as partners in God's creation. The Christian year calls us to spiritual mindfulness of the seasons of our lives. Boredom and burnout seldom characterize the experience of pastors who live in awareness of God's time amid our time. Prayerfully living the seasons of the Christian year devotionally as well as liturgically allows us to explore different dimensions of divine revelation in our lives.

Advent challenges us to awaken to images of hope amid a world that is anxious about many things: global warming, ecological disaster, economic uncertainty, and global political upheaval. In Advent, we ponder seeds of hope in unexpected places and embrace God's future for our lives and congregations.

Christmas invites us to see the world and our lives as incarnational in nature. Meister Eckhardt once stated that "all things are words of God." With the eyes of childhood, each day can be Christmas morning, each moment an incarnation of divine love. While the many pastoral demands of the Christmas season can deaden our spirits and raise our stress levels, vital ministry arises from a commitment to study and meditation even on the busiest days. We have found that the gentle days between Christmas and Epiphany provide an opportunity for retreat and reflection as well as rest and refreshment. Freed from day-to-day responsibilities during the twelve days of Christmas, we can experience Immanuel, "God with us," and set a spiritual tone for the days of rest and activity that stretch from Christmas to Epiphany.

Epiphany can awaken us to the many faces of God's revelation in our world. Epiphany challenges us to look for God's dynamic movement in all things and people. In every place, we can find magi bringing gifts. We can become surprising gift-givers to others. In what unlikely aspect of your life is divine revelation occurring? Pastoral transformation and vitality shine forth when we listen for God in the depths of our lives and, then, as Parker Palmer asserts, "let our lives speak."

Lent invites us to a different kind of contemplation and renewal, a type of withdrawal into "spacious simplicity" of the sort Jesus found in the desert. Like Jesus, we must "go away for awhile" to get our bearings and discern our vocation afresh. Although Lent can be a busy liturgical season for pastors, filled with extra services, visitation, ecumenical events, and potluck dinners, Lent also calls pastors to a time of retreat that will enable them to perceive blossoms bursting forth in the desert of our congregations and professional lives.

Holy Week can be a contemplative adventure as we experience the many faces of suffering and disease in our lives and the world. Once again, as during Lent, you are confronted with a choice: will you be overwhelmed by the sheer number of "special events" during Easter and Holy Week, or will you pause awhile to notice God's "sighs too deep for words" (Rom. 8:26) in their own pain and the cries of creation? Holy Week calls us to practice intentionality in our prayer lives regardless of our schedules. As one pastor notes, "During Holy Week, I was typically a spiritual wreck, constantly on the go, preparing for 'performances' on Maundy Thursday, Good Friday, and Easter. I was so busy that I neglected my own spiritual life until I finally decided to begin planning for Holy Week in February! These early hours of preparation enabled me to spend an hour each morning during Holy Week, meditating on the scriptures and going to the woods behind our home for prayer and solitude. I found myself walking with Jesus and gaining a new perspective on Jesus' suffering, death, and resurrection."

The season of *Easter* can and should awaken us to resurrection in new ways every year. As many of us look at our congregations and denominations, we ask, with Ezekiel, "can these dry bones live?" Easter reminds us that resurrection is always a possibility even for old and struggling congregations and denominations. Resurrection happens when and where we least expect it. Still, each Easter, with Wendell Berry, we are called to "practice resurrection" by allowing God to heal our negativity and show us a path forward when we see only a dead end.

Once again, it is essential for pastors to deepen their spirituality during the Easter season. As you prepare for your congregation's Easter celebration, we suggest that you consider taking a "Holy Saturday" quiet day in order to experience Easter morning with the uncertainty and joyful surprise the first followers of Jesus felt.

Pentecost is the lively season of the spirit that invites us to open to the surprising and fiery movements of God's spirit in our lives and congregations. During Pentecost, we encourage you to live imaginatively with the Acts of the Apostles, imaging God's healing breath and awakening fire permeating your own life.

Pentecost challenges you to go deeper in our faith and "become fire" as you dedicate yourself anew to feeding the flames of the pastoral fire within. During Pentecost, you can explore letting go of the narrow rationalism of the modern world and much liberal Christianity to embrace the deeper, nonrational dimensions of divine creativity in our world. Pentecost invites you to consider what miraculous events are still ahead for you and your congregation. We invite you during Pentecost to risk expecting great things from God, your congregants, and yourselves. It is a time to push on to new spiritual frontiers!

SACRED SPACE

In one of the great biblical stories, the patriarch Jacob goes to sleep with a stone for a pillow. During the night, he dreams of a "ladder of angels" ascending and descending from heaven, and he receives God's abundant and protective blessing. Jacob awakens, awestruck and disoriented, stammering out the affirmation, "Surely God was in this place—and I did not know it." Then, as he reflects more fully on his dream, Jacob exclaims in fear and awe, "How awesome is this place! This is none other than the house of God, and the gate of heaven!" (Gen. 28:10–17).

The practical meaning of divine omnipresence is that God is present wherever you are. This is a spatial as well as temporal promise. Even when you flee from God physically or spiritually, through busyness, addiction, self-justification, and denial of God's call to ministry, God is still with you. The God of Jacob promises us, "Know that I am with you and will keep you wherever you go." In a similar fashion, God's presence inspired the courage of Esther and Mary the mother of Jesus, and can inspire you today, if you let it!

Take a moment to read Genesis 28:10–17 again. Did you notice that the angels first "ascend" from earth to heaven? While this passage has many symbolic meanings and can be read from a variety of angles, surely one meaning is that God is with us in this world as well as in the heavenly spheres. The place where we are right now is Beth-el, the home of God. Could we already be in heaven and not be aware of it? Where is your Beth-el? Where do you find yourself uncomfortably "sleeping" with only a stone for a pillow?

Although God is present wherever we are, each of us needs to awaken to God's presence by finding our own sacred times and places. As you look at your life, do you have a sacred place? If not, where might you find such a holy place? The Celts called such places "thin places"—where the divine and human, the Creative One and the creation, are somehow spiritually synchronized. As you ponder the nearness of the cosmic God, where do you find God's presence most fully? For some pastors, it is their study, a favorite chair, a meditation room, or place of retreat, such as a nearby lake or the seashore, or a holy spot such as Iona, Ghost Ranch, Ring Lake Ranch, the National Cathedral, or Findhorn. For others, God's space and time meet as they gently hold a sleeping child or read on their back porch at sunset.

Jacob experienced God's presence in a dream at Beth-el, but God promises to be with him everywhere he travels. That is God's promise to us as well. When we discover God in one holy or "thin" place, it is easier to discover that all places can share in God's revelation, even an intensive care unit or emergency room. We are always at home, even when we are pilgrims.

Renewed and renewing vital ministry involves the transformation space and time. When you can hold your holy place within, you will discover God in the simple moments and regular tasks of ministry and in the awesome spaces of ministry, and all places and times will become *kairos*-laden. We will experience the lively power that comes from living in the Holy Here and Holy Now.

FEEDING THE MINISTERIAL FIRE

Vital and transformative ministry is the gift of God's abundant life. Spiritual teachers suggest that there are two contrasting ways of looking at the world—through the fearful eyes of scarcity or spacious perception of abundance. Threatened by busyness and time-sickness, you are challenged to live in light of God's everlasting life in every here and now. Awakened to lifelines, rather than deadlines, you will have enough time to minister with grace and calm despite your busy calendar. You will let go of your sense of urgency in light of the God's moment-by-moment and lifelong vision. Living by abundance, you will have enough time to integrate in a creative and life-giving way congregational leadership, family life, personal spirituality, and care for justice and planetary well-being.

A Holistic Spiritual Practice

Meditation is one of the antidotes to the hurry sickness that leads to burnout. The regular practice of meditative prayer, whether centering prayer, transcendental meditation, or prayer of the heart, calms us mentally, physiologically, and spiritually. Time virtually stands still when we are aligned with God's presence in meditative prayer. As you seek to transform time by opening to God's everlasting life in the moments of your life, we suggest you explore the practice of quiet prayer in the spirit of the Society of Friends, or Quakers.

Quakers believe that God's inner light shines in all things and that there is something of God in every creature. Joining theology, spirituality, and social action, the Quakers experienced God's presence in indigenous peoples, convicts, and slaves. This vision was translated into acts of justice and shalom.

Take a few minutes to meditate on Psalm 46:10, "be still and know that I am God." Then simply take a few moments to "be still" in God's presence. Take time to listen to God's voice in the sheer silence. If your mind wanders or you are distracted by your environment, simply return to the silence as you remember that God is your deepest reality and that God's light constantly enlightens you.

A Practice for Healthy Ministry

In the days ahead, take time to become aware of your response to the times of your life. When you experience yourself feeling busy as a result of your schedule, take a moment, first, to breathe deeply. You may choose to sit in a quiet place or take a prayer walk. After you have found a place of centeredness, take time to look at your daily, weekly, or monthly schedule. What events are essential to your personal mission, family, professional, and self-care responsibilities? What events are optional? What "due dates" are mandatory and what others can be renegotiated?

The ability to say "yes" and "no" wholeheartedly to opportunities for ministry is essential to vital and healthy spiritual leadership. Halfheartedness not only leads to poor performance but also quenches the fires of vital ministry. Begin to practice healthy self-differentiation by saying "no" to events that do not reflect your life mission and vocation. While all pastors have "duty calls" or responsibilities that simply come with our pastoral roles, a commitment to healthy and vital ministry requires us to make time-related decisions with intentionality. Although saying "no" may disappoint some of your colleagues and parishioners, in the long run a schedule that reflects your deepest mission and the mission of your congregations and family will add zest and vitality to every aspect of your life.

An Affirmation of Faith

Your attitude toward time is a matter of faith and can either enhance your health or diminish your well-being. The quality of your ministry depends on a sense of spaciousness even when your schedule is full. The following affirmations regularly repeated throughout the day will transform your attitude toward time.

- I dwell in God's everlasting life.
- I have all the time and energy I need to serve God and fulfill my personal and professional mission.
- I experience God's calm and peace every moment of the day.

A Covenant of Wholeness and Vitality in Ministry

More than once, in this text, we have stated that, although pastors cannot manage time, they can be intentional about their attitudes toward time and their use of the time in their lives. Counting your days in light of God's everlasting life awakens you to the wonder of time. In light of this, you may choose to make a covenant with God and yourself, such as the following:

- I covenant to take time for rest, recreation, and study.

- I covenant to make decisions and commitments in light of my personal and professional mission and calling.

- I covenant to be aware of my experience of time and to slow down prayerfully whenever I begin to experience time anxiety.

SIX

TRANSFORMING RELATIONSHIPS

n the course of writing this book, our only child, Matthew, age twenty-seven, was diagnosed with germ cell cancer. Within forty-eight hours after the diagnosis, he received calls, e-mails, and visits from friends across the country. As we rushed to support Matt and his wife, Ingrid, we knew that we also needed a "team" of friends, family, and colleagues to help us get through the stress of diagnosis and treatment. We picked up the phone and wrote e-mails, asking for prayer and personal support from friends and professional colleagues as well as denominational judicatory officials. We knew that our ability to support our son and his wife of just three months depended on the support of a network of friends who came with food, hugs, cards, calls, and stories of how they or one of their family members survived cancer. We could not fulfill our vocations as parents of an adult child as well as our professional responsibilities with strength and insight without the prayers, words, and touch of faithful friends and colleagues. In the first months following the diagnosis, our family experienced firsthand the meaning of healthy interdependence as we sought to balance creatively our personal and professional lives. We needed to feed the fires of parental support and professional excellence with the fuel of healthy relationships.

Our lives are profoundly relational. Whether we speak of the interdependence of life, described by ecologists and Christian and Buddhist mystics, or the biblical image of the body of Christ, we are constantly shaped by, and shape, our environment. Long before contemporary physics, family systems theory, environmental ethics, and process-relational theology, the Hebraic community recognized that it is not good for a person to be alone and that a good life requires the partnership of healthy and holy otherness (Gen. 2:18).

As spiritual leaders, we find wholeness, vitality, and fulfillment in healthy relatedness, whether it is in a committed lifelong relationship, a spiritual friendship, mentoring, collegial support, or faithful friends. When relationships bring healing and wholeness, we can exclaim with our Hebraic forebears, "this at last is bone of my bone and flesh of my flesh" (Gen. 2:23). Vitality, health, and spiritual growth in ministry find their foundation in personal and professional relationships that nurture, inspire, challenge, support, and provide perspective.

Our son's diagnosis with cancer called us to be intentional about what we had often taken for granted, the giving and receiving of love that characterizes healthy professional and personal relationships. As Bruce sought to balance a two-hour drive from Lancaster, Pennsylvania, to Washington, D.C., overnight stays in Washington during chemotherapy weeks, a busy schedule of administrative and teaching duties at the seminary, and sermons at our congregation, he was reminded of another "holy trinity" necessary for a well-lived and dynamic pastoral life—*faith, family,* and *vocation.* Ministerial vitality and excellence involves a dynamic interdependence of these three values, each of which takes precedence at one time or another during a pastor's career. Kate felt that same holy trinity as she split her time equally between organizing medical appointments, chemotherapy treatments, shopping, and taking care of domestic details for Matt and Ingrid along with pastoral care and leadership in our congregation. Gracefully, both the seminary and our congregation allowed us to be parents as well as pastors and academics.

When we use the term "family," we refer the dynamic give and take of committed partners, whether heterosexual or homosexual, and close and supportive friends and relatives. These relationships reflect what Martin Buber described as the "holy otherness," without which we cannot discover our own gifts and passions. While "vocation," narrowly speaking, refers to our calling as spiritual leaders in congregations, campuses, hospitals, and other contexts, it also refers to day-to-day responsibilities and encounters that call us to do something creative and beautiful for God. It is our *faith*, that is, our experience of the Holy and commitment to embodying that experience through spiritual practices, self-awareness, ethical relationships, and social and planetary concern, that inspires the ever-changing dance of a healthy, lively, and transforming personal and pastoral life.

In the pages that follow, our goal is to reflect briefly upon how healthy relatedness can bring vitality, transformation, and insight to the practice of ministry. We will lift up the importance of a variety of healthy relationships that nurture and guide a well-lived and vital pastoral ministry. Although our goal is not to write a treatise on committed relationships or communication skills, we believe values such as affection, respect, equality, healthy communication, fidelity, forgiveness, gratitude, and celebration are essential components of the healthy relationships necessary for a vital ministry. In the following sections, we will focus on the role of committed lifelong relationships, parenting, personal and professional relationships, and spiritual friendships in feeding the fire of ministry.

INTIMACY AND ENERGY

In Plato's dialogue the *Symposium*, the philosopher writes of a time in which the human body was spherical, possessing four legs and four arms. Because of the pride of these first humans, the gods cut each sphere in half, creating today's human race. Now, according to Plato, our lives are spent trying to find the spiritual half that will complete our lives. Love is, accordingly, not only the quest for unity, the re-uniting of the separated spheres, but also the quest for wholeness that gives energy, direction, and meaning to our lives.

Committed relationships, whether we describe them in terms of marriages, holy unions, or lifelong partnerships, are intended to add to the beauty, joy, and purpose of our lives. While single persons can also find wholeness and vitality in their personal and professional lives, marriage and other committed relationships can be the source of new and creative spiritual and relational energies that transform the totality of our lives, most especially our vocations as pastors. Our committed relationships are themselves vocations that enable us to see God in the mirror of those whom we love.

While we realize that our relationship as a clergy couple is somewhat unique among ordained persons, we recognize that for nearly thirty years of marriage we have mentored, taught, consoled, advised, and energized each other. We have edited each other's sermons, supported each other in congregational conflict, and advised each other on the merits of accepting a particular congregational or academic call. Indeed, this book is the fruit of a lifelong partnership that has ripened into our current coministry, leadership in ministerial excellence and spiritual formation groups, writing, and workshop leadership. While we have often stumbled in our personal and professional partnerships, our commitment to joining spiritual practices, parenting, relational growth, and service to God has enabled our marriage and professional lives to bear abundant fruit for ourselves, congregations, seminaries, and friends.

Still, despite the vitality, direction, and refreshment a healthy relationship brings to ministry, today's pastors must be highly intentional in practicing the arts of relational wholeness in ministry. Too many successful pastors have burned out or are suffering from brownout because they have neglected to nurture loving relationships that are the wellspring of a flourishing life. When he was ordained, Robert embraced a theology of ministry built upon the foundation of loving God first, the church second, and family third. In his life and ministry, serving God and loving his wife Julie were almost always at odds. Throughout their marriage, Julie often complained ironically that "Robert was really married to the church and I was his mistress. Robert preached and led worship on holidays—Christmas Eve and Christmas morning with four services were the worst. If there was a minor emergency, he abandoned me and the children at the dinner table and often cut short family vacations. Every time the phone rang, I knew he would be gone in a few minutes. Can't Robert love God, the church, and me all at once? I realize I have to make sacrifices for God and the church, but not all the time. I felt like I couldn't challenge his priorities, because obviously God came first!"

When Julie finally put her foot down and threatened Robert with divorce, Robert woke up to what was really happening in his life. "I was living in two worlds—God's and my family's—and I forgotten that God called me to be a husband and father as well as a pastor. It's been difficult, but I am learning to trust that God will use my staff and the lay leaders to do ministry so that I can spend more time with Julie and the kids."

Healthy and vital ministry is grounded in a holistic theology that is embodied in the arts of relational wholeness. Grounded in a vision of divine omnipresence and the interdependence of life, we affirm that there is no dualism between loving God and loving our families. In the spirit of the dance of the Holy Trinity, we live one integrated life, in which our constantly changing concrete priorities are always shaped by our commitment to God's aim at wholeness. In a world of relationships, we love God by loving our families. The love we have for each other—embracing children, friends, congregants, and the world—is one way we can add to the beauty of the world.

A healthy and vital pastor, able to energize and inspire her or his congregation over the long haul, recognizes that he or she has many vocations —spouse or partner, parent, friend, citizen, pastor—all of which can bring glory to God and beauty to the world. An energetic and transformative ministry is intimately connected to the arts of relational wholeness—time, affirmation, communication, and vision.

Time for Commitment

Throughout this book, we have asserted the importance of time in ministry. The mystical experiences that inspired and set apart the first priests, healers, and spirit-persons involved sacred time and sacred space. Transforming relatedness, whether in a committed lifelong relationship or in parenting, involves creating a "sanctuary of time" in which healthy and vital relationships can flourish.[1] Too often, however, pastors and their committed partners admit that they do not spend enough time together. When they take time for one another, it is often hurried, interrupted, and insufficient to rekindle the flames of intimacy and love. Our professional lives take on new vitality and purpose when we recognize that we are called to become fire in our committed relationships as well as in our ministries.

During the first few weeks after our son's diagnosis with cancer, the primary attention of our daily lives turned from our relationship as a couple to his well-being and the well-being of his wife Ingrid. Recognizing that couples tend to grow apart when their children are in crisis, we worked hard to stay in touch with each other through phone calls when one of us stayed with Matt and Ingrid, maintained our walking ritual as much as possible, and cancelled certain congregational and seminary meetings so that we could have a few more hours together. At Kate's request, Bruce chose to stay home with her one weekend rather than travel to the west coast for an academic meeting. We realized that we needed time together in order to have the energy and calm to respond creatively to our son and his wife in this time of illness. We also knew that times set apart for conversation and play, even in this critical time in our son's life, would enable us to continue to preach, teach, and pastor effectively.

Lillian and David, a clergy couple like ourselves, take Mondays off together. Often they just sit in front of the fire or on their deck, reading and enjoying snacks and coffee. Other times, they go to museums or art galleries. While they avoid talking more than necessary about the details of their professional lives on their days off, often they share theological and homiletical insights or ideas from books they are reading. They note that these days off inspire and energize them relationally and professionally for the rest of the week.

When Alice recognized that the birth of her second child, along with a growing congregation, might leave her little time for her marriage to a high school music teacher, she decided to take Friday and Sunday evenings for time with her husband. They typically hire a child-care person and go to dinner or a movie. They take time to look at their schedules at the beginning of each month as a way of affirming the importance of each one's vocation as well as the priority of the marriage and parenting. Further, Alice works hard not to schedule Saturday meetings and only takes on a handful of weddings each year in order preserve Saturdays as family and sermon "touch-up" days. Alice notes that these family and relational times together "refresh and relax me. I always seem to problem solve better at church after a date with Jim."

Paul and his committed partner Charles, an architect, take one night each month to go to a bed and breakfast and pursue their interest in American history. Paul notes that "these monthly getaways not only strengthen our relationship but give me a larger perspective on my ministry. It is easy to become myopic in ministry, but our mutual interest in American history and our monthly overnights together make my professional problems less important and consuming of my attention."

In her description of her mother's final illness, French author Simone de Beauvior notes that the world had shrunk to the size of her mother's hospital room. While there are times in which we must focus primarily on one thing in our lives, healthy ministry is grounded in relationships and avocations that lie outside the congregation. Although our committed partners may often have roles in the congregation where we pastor and may be a source of comfort and counsel for us in our professional lives, healthy relatedness helps us to experience the church and our ministries as one of our many callings as well as one of many places where God is revealing Godself in the world. Ironically, the greater our sense of God's presence beyond the church through hobbies and healthy and committed relationships of all kinds, the wiser and more effective our congregational ministries will become. It is clear to us, both from our own tried and tested marriage of nearly thirty years and from our observation of other healthy clergy marriages, that growing and lively relationships beyond the church enhance the health and vitality of our spiritual leadership and serve as an antidote to enmeshed and codependent relationships within the church.

The Affirmative Marriage

In his Letter to Philippians, the apostle Paul invites this early Christian congregation to live affirmatively in both their relationships and their personal lives:

> Whatever is true, whatever is honorable, whatever is just, whatever
> is pure, whatever is pleasing, whatever is commendable, if there is

any excellence and if there is anything worthy of praise, think about these things . . . and the God of peace will be with you. (Phil. 4:8–9)

Our personal self-talk and interpersonal conversations shape our lives, relationships, and vision of reality. The apostle Paul affirms that, in contrast to the negativity and scarcity thinking that shapes many of our personal and professional lives, "God will fully satisfy every need of yours according to his riches in glory in Christ Jesus" (Phil. 4:19). A transformed mind and transformed language lead to transformed personal and professional lives.

Heather and Aaron discovered that changing the words they spoke to one another was essential to the healing of their marriage. After several years of marriage, they were so preoccupied in their busyness of balancing professional lives in ministry and medicine that they barely had time to talk to one another. When they spoke, their words were often critical, angry, and impatient. Instead of seeing the holiness in one another, they saw the imperfections in each other. They were on the verge of separation until they made a commitment to transform their words and images of one another. A Presbyterian pastor, Heather was spiritually convicted when she realized that she treated everyone who attended her church with the kindness due to a beloved child of God, except her husband, Aaron. Aaron came to the same conclusion when he realized that he gave his patients the benefit of the doubt but was constantly assuming the worst in terms of his wife's behavior. He came to realize that his calling as a healer extended to his family and marriage as well as his patients.

According to Heather, "When we began to use simple words like 'please' and 'thank you,' our relationship began to change." From that small beginning, they chose to point out the positive rather than negative aspects of their relationship. After a few months, Heather realized something amazing. She felt a sense of peace both at home and at the church. "Six months ago," Heather confesses, "I felt stressed out throughout the day. I carried the stress of my marriage to church each morning. Now I leave home happy and arrive at church feeling blessed." In addition to changing their language, Aaron and Heather both sought personal and marriage counseling. Today, their healthy marriage brings joy and vitality to their professional lives and parenting.

We experienced the same transformation by practicing "attitudinal healing" to heal our own marriage. After several years of marriage, our marriage was at a crossroads. One marriage counselor even pronounced our marriage "dead." As we struggled to be good parents to our young son Matt, we made a commitment to live by abundance rather than scarcity in our marriage. In the spirit of attitudinal healing, we chose to look for the "light rather than the lampshade" in one another. We practiced seeing and then bringing forth angels when previously we focused on the boulders of each others' lives. We shared a daily journal, spoke words of loving affirmation, and discovered the power of forgiveness to transform the past and open the future to new possibilities of intimacy and commitment. The healing of our marriage opened up new energies for professional energy, writing, and parenting.[2]

Our leadership in ministerial excellence and spiritual transformation groups and our current vital and successful cominstry can be attributed to the affirmations that healed our marriage over two decades ago. Like many other clergy couples who have experienced healing through affirmative words and behavior, the positive energy of our marriage brings creativity to our academic and congregational ministries. Our ability to be a cohesive and loving, albeit imperfect, team in responding to the personal, professional, and family stresses of our son's illness had its roots in our commitment to see the holy in one another.

Looking Together in the Same Direction

A strong spiritual and communal vision is at the heart of vital, creative, and healthy ministry. Vision is also at the heart of healthy and life-supporting committed relationships. We believe that God has a flexible, evolving, and open-ended vision for our personal and relational lives as well as our ministries. In contrast to Rick Warren's assertion in *The Purpose Driven Life* that God plans the most important details of our lives without our input, we believe that divine providence is a matter of "call and response." God presents us with a vision for each moment as well as for the long haul and calls us to embody our personal, professional, and communal visions in our own unique and faithful way.

Without a vision, or a sense of mission, a congregation, couple, or pastor will flounder amid the conflicting demands of life. When our son was diagnosed with cancer, we were called as parents to place his well-being and the well-being of his spouse as central to our lives as a couple. Our vision of life as couple was embodied in numerous visits to Washington, D.C., over a three-month period, research on physicians, house cleaning and shopping, and consideration for Ingrid and Matt's privacy. It was also embodied in our ongoing commitment to Kate's ninety-year-old mother and Bruce's handicapped brother.

Our marriage vision resembles a statement attributed to Antoine de Saint-Exupery, "love is looking outward together in the same direction." As we look toward the same horizon as a couple, as partners in writing, ministry, and consulting, and as parents, we are guided by shared spiritual disciplines, a commitment to consulting with one another over major decisions, and a willingness to reach out to the larger community. As a couple, we have made a commitment to place God's vision at the heart of our own personal visions and to be faithful not only to one another in marriage and family life but to God's calling in ministry and service.

Implicitly or explicitly, every couple has a mission and lives by a vision. The challenge for clergy couples is to be intentional about both formulating and living by a shared vision. A shared vision is especially important for professional couples, whether clergy couples or ministers in long-term committed relationships with professionals in other fields, since the tendency of professionals is to give more attention to their jobs than to their relationships and families. Living by a vision, creatively grounded in God's vision for our life and ministry, enables us to prioritize and find direction amid the many demands of a pastor's life.

Visionary relationships add energy and direction to ministry even when they call pastors to spend less time on church-related work or leave the church early for date nights and family nights. Visionary relationships enable pastors to be whole-hearted rather than divided in their faithfulness to their ministerial calling. Recognizing that God has given pastors many possible callings and many visions for their lives enables pastors to be fully present to the divine calling embedded in each particular task and responsibility whether at home with the family, taking time for prayer and retreat, or working faithfully for congregational transformation and vitality.

As you look at your relationship, what is its primary vision? What common mission do you have as a couple? How does this vision shape your relationship and time commitments? For Susan, a Presbyterian pastor, and her husband, Dave, an engineer, their vision was to raise "healthy, loving, and socially responsible children." For Charlie and Yvonne, a clergy couple in midlife, their corporate vision was to join their love of nature with activism in responding to global warming. Remember, embracing a flexible and dynamic vision provides direction and guidance for everyday decisions, both large and small.

POSITIVE PARENTING

In her insightful narrative of ministry in a South Bronx Lutheran congregation, Heidi Neumark describes what often happens when a pastor forgets to balance pastoral ministry with family life.

> When she was three years old, Ana locked herself in a closet, clutching a bag of her outgrown clothes. She had heard me say that I was going to take them to church. She hadn't minded me giving them away until she knew where they were going. I guess she felt she'd shared enough with the church by having to share her mother.[3]

Pastoral ministry is by its very nature a laboratory for creative multitasking. Sadly, children often get left out in the course of a pastor's multitasking. As one pastor notes, "I barely have an opportunity to see my baby. I drop her off at the babysitter's house on my way to church, pick her up for dinner at home, and often rush off to a meeting for the rest of the night. Weekends aren't any better. With weddings, sermons, and youth group, I feel like I see some of parishioners more than I see my own child." Thankfully, this pastor awakened to the possibility of transformed relationships with her family and congregation. She discovered that the flexibility of a minister's week can be a blessing as well as a curse. After taking a seminar for new pastors on "time and ministry," sponsored by Lancaster Theological Seminary, she notes that "I was determined to change my life and be more attentive to my baby. I didn't want to miss out on his first words and steps. Now, if there's no emergency at church, I come home every afternoon to play and nap with my baby. When I informed the chair of the board that I was going to cut back on evening meetings in order to spend more time at home with my husband and baby, his response surprised me—he felt my job as a parent and spouse was just as important as my ministry to the church."

At the heart of this book is the affirmation that ministerial creativity, vitality, and insight are a whole-person enterprise, embracing mind, body, spirit, and relationships. Healthy parenting adds zest and liveliness to ministry by connecting us to the primal wellsprings of human relatedness—the flow of life from ourselves to others from generation to generation.

Our attitudes toward time shape our parenting along with every other aspect of ministry. "Quality time" is grounded in "quantity time." Some of our best moments in parenting have happened as one of us drove our child to school, played catch in the backyard, read bedtime stories, or simply sat beside him watching a children's program on television or a sporting event. As our son received treatments for cancer from October 2007 to January 2008, our "best times" involved watching movies at the oncology infusion clinic, conversations on spirituality and marriage, sitting at dinner with his wife, Ingrid, and giving him reiki treatments to promote his overall well-being.[4]

While pastors can be interrupted by emergencies at any moment of the day, it is essential that they intentionally set aside time for their children throughout the week, giving their role as parents as high a priority as the youth group, choir practice, or ministerium. Pastors need to remind themselves constantly that their schedules are often a matter of choice as well as necessity. Further, certain "emergencies" can wait for us to finish dinner or read a bedtime story with our child. As one pastor noted, "Before our child was born, I said 'yes' to every request from the denominational district superintendent. But now I am more selective in my responses. I realize that when I say 'yes' to one request, I am saying 'no' to something else, whether it be playing hide and seek or watching *Sesame Street* with my toddler. Nowadays, I think twice before adding one more thing to my schedule. I ask myself, 'is this activity more important to God and to my ministry than being with family?'"

Vital and healthy parenting calls us to greater self-awareness. In remembering our own childhoods in the course of parenting, we are challenged to seek our own personal transformation and healing. Even the happiest childhood is ambiguous—while there is often much for which to be grateful, there are also scars and habits that we need to address if we are to be healthy parents and pastors. As congregational systems theory notes, remembering our childhood and the roles we adopted in our families can be a source of liberation, self-differentiation, and effectiveness in our pastoral ministries. Surely the same is true for our vocation as parents. More than once, we have caught ourselves repeating unhealthy as well as healthy patterns of behavior we learned in our respective families of origin. Such discoveries have led to painful and healing conversations with one another, with spiritual directors, friends, and therapists. As parents, we are challenged to "be not conformed to this world"—the world of our family of origin—"but be transformed by the renewing of our minds" (Rom. 12:2).

Commitment to professional and relational transformation brings with it an equal commitment to listening to our children. Psychologists point out the importance of "mirroring" in a child's healthy growth. As parents, our vocation is to *pause, notice, open, yield,* and *respond* to our children's experiences as revelations of God in our midst. The God who speaks through all things surely speaks through the cooing, crying, and calling of our children. In honoring our children's experiences at every stage of life as holy, even as we honor our own need for interpersonal boundaries and appropriate behaviors at home, we are deepening both our own spiritual center as well as our children's spiritual and emotional lives. We are teaching them self-differentiation and self-worth in the course of our own strengthening of our own healthy self-differentiation and affirmation of self-worth. Our own balance of mirroring, intimacy, and personal centeredness with our children is symbiotically related to the same balance in our congregational ministries.

Healthy parenting is a spiritual practice, joining self-awareness, self-differentiation, mirroring and listening, forgiveness, celebration, playfulness, and love. As we can attest, the joy of parenting, even in times of sickness and challenge, radiates through our whole ministries, enabling us to minister effectively and energetically as whole and integrated persons who call our own congregations to that same experience of wholeness and integration.

TRANSFORMING RELATEDNESS

Personal and professional relationships add vitality and stature to a minister's life and practice, and respond to the loneliness that many pastors experience, especially in small town and rural congregations. Isolated pastors often become so enmeshed in the challenges of their congregations that they have few interests or relationships beyond the church. Small issues take on epic proportions in the apparently "closed system" world of congregational life. With only congregational relationships to sustain them, many pastors find themselves, on the one hand, devoting themselves completely to church life and, on the other hand, feeling resentful at the monotony of day-o-day congregational existence. Like Zacchaeus, pastors need to "climb a tree" in order to gain perspective on their ministries and place their lives in a larger spiritual and global context. Holy relationships liberate pastors from enmeshment in their congregations, awaken emotional and intellectual energies, and provide guidance and inspiration for the day-to-day and long-term practice of healthy and vital ministry. In this section, we will briefly explore three types of holy friendships that nurture and transform ministry—personal friendships, spiritual direction, and professional colleague groups.

The Joy of Friendship

In the wake of our son's diagnosis of cancer, we knew that we couldn't make it alone. We called upon friends and colleagues from every season of our lives, from the early days of our marriage and professional lives to our recent move to Lancaster, Pennsylvania. Our friends supported and sustained us with visits, gifts, prayers, notes, e-mails, and personal touch.

Healthy friendships, ranging beyond the congregation, are essential to vital and creative ministry. On the one hand, healthy friendships expand our vision of the world beyond congregational and vocational life. Like the lilies of the field, they often "neither toil nor spin," but simply add richness, diversity, and contrast to our experience. The joy of friendship is a grace in which we can be ourselves, receiving and giving, with no need to perform, succeed, or achieve. Embodying grace at its best, healthy friendships enable us simply to become our fullest selves, regardless of our current professional situation.

Once again, ministry best flourishes when it is not the *only* focal point of our lives. God comes to us in the voice of a friend, in a simple touch, in the willingness of another to go the second mile, and in challenge and counsel. Perhaps the power of friendship, given and received, is found in the fact that we don't have to *do* anything or require special behavior from the "holy other." Friendship reminds us that spiritual growth may occur in times of play as well as prayer, in partying as well as petition, in conversation as well as contemplation. Like the birds of the air and the lilies of the field, friendship allows us to experience the divine in the ordinary human acts of eating, drinking, and playing. Authentic friendship reminds us that pastors often experience God most fully when they aren't "on duty." In the spirit of the Shaker song "Simple Gifts," the simplicity of graceful friendships turns us toward God even when we do not invoke the name of God or try to do anything special on God's behalf.

In a time in which pastors are called to practice appropriate relational boundaries, healthy friendships provide the emotional intimacy pastors need so that they can minister to their congregants without emotional enmeshment or the need for intimacy from parishioners. While pastors will always experience appropriate closeness, and sometimes love, toward certain congregants, the expansive nature of noncongregational friendships along with committed relationships enables us to love well and rightly in our congregations. Further, the variety of perspectives gained from clergy and nonclergy friends helps pastors look at their ministries from new perspectives. Lively and healthy friendships energize pastors personally and professionally and support innovative and faithful ministry over the long haul.

Spiritual Friendships

Today, many Protestant ministers are experiencing the wisdom and growth that comes from their covenant to enter into a relationship with a spiritual friend or director. Typically, these pastors meet monthly with a wise and experienced guide who keeps before them their quest to be open to God in their personal and professional lives. As strange as it may seem, many pastors fail to be intentional about their own spiritual lives. Like the laity they seek to inspire, they often don't take time for daily prayer and meditation, retreat, devotional reading, or other spiritual practices. Eventually, such pastors find that their ministries become stale, superficial, and stressful.

A commitment to spiritual direction constantly places before the pastor the question "Where are you experiencing God in your life and ministry?"

Intentional spiritual reflection enables pastors to see their professional and personal lives as part of a larger spiritual journey in which every activity reveals the presence of God. As one pastor affirms, "Whenever I have a serious decision to make in my life, I ask my partner and a few close friends for their counsel and opinions. But I also take my concern prayerfully to my spiritual director. She never gives me advice or shares her own opinion. Instead, she prays with me and points me back to God. She asks me to attend to God's wisdom present within my personal and professional life. As I spend time in silence with her, I gain perspective on the challenges of church life and sometimes even experience God's presence in the difficult people in my congregation." Another pastor reflects, "Before I began spiritual direction, my spirituality was inch deep and random, at best. I prayed during worship and at meetings, but seldom took time to draw near to God. My director held me accountable to a spiritual practice that emerged from my particular personality and lifestyle. Since beginning regular spiritual direction, I experience a sense of presence that binds together my personal and professional life in a healthy way. People comment that my preaching has greater insight and depth, and that I'm not as rattled when conflict emerges in board meetings."

In individual or group spiritual direction, pastors find new perspectives on their lives, commit themselves to regular spiritual practices, and learn to distinguish between the trivial and the important in ministry and personal life. In pausing to attend and then respond to the Spirit's "sighs too deep for words," pastors grow in wisdom, stature, and energy for vital and transforming ministry that inspires their congregations to grow in spiritual depth and commitment.[5]

Professional Friendships

The first Monday of every month for nearly a decade, eight pastors gather for breakfast in the back room of a local restaurant in western Maryland. Although their explicit goal is to explore the lectionary readings for the month ahead, this informal collegial group has grown into a spiritual and professional support group that transcends age, denomination, and gender. Each gathering begins with a time of prayer and checking in. Over the years, participants have supported each other through congregational crises, individual dark nights of the soul, personal illness and illness in the family, and professional questioning. Though this group is informal in nature, with no explicit convener or institutional support, participants covenant to support and keep confidence with one another. As one participant notes, "Over the years, this group has kept me out of trouble in my personal and professional life. I know that I can take the floor and share about a conflict with a parishioner and receive guidance that will help me do the right thing. I also know that seven other people will be praying for me during the week. My sermons are a lot better because of this group, and so is my life and ministry. I know I'm not alone, and when I'm struggling with an issue, I can pick up the phone and call one of my colleagues."

Just a few miles away, a group of retired pastors and their spouses also meet monthly for food, fellowship, and support as they seek to live creatively beyond full-time ministry. Many of them have known each other as colleagues and friends for decades and as they progress through life's final season, they support one another in sickness and health, bereavement and celebration. Whether formal or informal, it is essential for pastors to find colleagues with whom to share their lives in a safe and supportive context.

Thanks to the generosity and inspiration of the Lilly Endowment, seminaries and denominations across the country have initiated groups for pastoral excellence and support.[6] At Lancaster Theological Seminary, Bruce directs ministerial excellence and spiritual formation programs for every season of ministry—first congregational call following seminary graduation; mid-career in ministry; and prior to retirement. The goal of these groups is to provide pastors with a safe collegial environment within which to grow in ministerial identity, learn practices of spiritual growth and self-care, share insights and counsel, continue their theological education, and explore how to live out their calling faithfully in their unique professional season.

The Wholeness in Ministry program provides small and large group collegial support, continuing education, and spiritual formation for pastors in their first call following graduation from seminary. Participants meet in small groups three times each year to explore issues in pastoral ministry such as self-care, money, conflict resolution, grief in ministry, strategic planning, personal integrity, and preaching in the context of a prayerful, supportive environment. In addition, participants in this three-year program have the opportunity to gather for three or four plenary meetings each year, aimed at ongoing theological and professional education in areas such as coaching in ministry, the postmodern church, survival after death, music in the small church, Sabbath time, and the spirituality of administration. Following the same format, Renewing Ministry groups gather pastors with more than five years of experience over a three-year period for spiritual formation, theological education, and support as they seek to be catalysts for the ongoing transformation of their congregations and professional lives. Harvesting Wisdom meets three times over a six-month period as a means of supporting pastors over sixty years of age as they seek to "finish well" in full-time ministry. Harvesting Wisdom groups provide a context for a preretirement vision quest in which experienced pastors remember their calls; celebrate their ministries; let go of wounds, mistakes, and grievances; and explore the next stages of their professional and personal journeys. These ministerial excellence groups are inspired by Paul's affirmation in Philippians: "I am confident of this, that the one who began a good work among you will bring it to completion by the day of Jesus Christ. . . . the harvest of righteousness that comes through Jesus Christ for the glory and praise of God" (Phil. 1:6,11). Pastors who participate in intentional colleague groups bear abundant fruit that nurtures their congregations and relationships.[7]

FEEDING THE MINISTERIAL FIRE

Transforming relationships are intimately connected with the spiritual practices of creative interdependence and gratitude.

A Holistic Spiritual Practice

In this exercise, set aside thirty minutes for contemplation. Begin by simply sitting in a quiet place, resting in God's ever-present gracefulness. Take a few deep centering and calming breaths. As you continue gently breathing, begin to visualize the faces of your loved ones—spouse, parents, children, friends, mentors—one by one. Experience God's presence as you look deeply into their faces. In the spirit of intercession, imagine each of your loved ones surrounded and permeated by God's healing and empowering light. Before moving on the next person, take a moment to give thanks for your relationship and the unique gift it brings to your life.

Contemplation, as Thomas Merton notes, is intimately related to action. Make a commitment to contact through e-mail, phone, or a personal visit each of the persons for whom you pray. As part of your ongoing relational spiritual formation, regularly pray for each of your loved ones and closest friends, integrating in your prayers intercession and thanksgiving in your care for them.

A Practice for Healthy Ministry

As we faced our son's diagnosis with cancer, we knew that we could not "go around" this diagnosis or avoid the challenges of the medical care he received. We had to "go through" this dark valley with one another and our son and his wife. We also realized that as healthy and energetic as our committed relationship was, we could not sustain ourselves or flourish individually and as a couple during this difficult healing period apart from reaching out to friends. We were filled with gratitude at the generosity of our friends and made a commitment to be as supportive to them, should they be faced with a personal or family crisis.

In this spirit, take some time to reflect on the nature of your friendships. Whom, if anyone, would you call upon in a time of profound personal, professional, or spiritual need? Whom do you currently call upon simply for a good conversation or to spend time in graceful play and relaxation? Take time to express your gratitude explicitly to your friends. If you have been neglecting a close friendship due to the rigors of ministry or the demands of family life, take a moment to write an e-mail, make a phone call, or arrange for a get-together.

Are there persons with whom you would like a deeper friendship? In what ways might you reach out to nurture a new friendship? Friendships are not optional in ministry, but are essential to lively, healthy, and devoted ministry over the long haul.

An Affirmation of Faith

Friendship and committed relationships inspire and are built upon our spiritual affirmations. As we focus affirmatively on holy relationships, they deepen and bring greater insight and joy to our lives. We suggest that you focus on the following affirmations as a way of deepening your relationships in such a way that they complement and add zest to your professional life.

- I give and receive love in all my relationships.

- I am open to God's grace in every relationship.

- I see God's presence and bring it forth in every relationship.

A Covenant of Wholeness and Vitality in Ministry

Healthy relatedness is a matter of commitment and intentionality. Vital and healthy ministry is a matter of seeing our relationships as essential to our spiritual growth and calling as God's beloved children. Our vocation as pastors is energized when we awaken to God's vocational call in our committed relationships, parenting, friendships, and collegial relationships. The following covenants will help you to balance professional excellence with healthy relatedness.

- I make a commitment to sharing my heart with my loved ones.

- I make a commitment to praying for my loved ones, children, and friends.

- I commit myself to spending holy time with my friends and family.

SEVEN

STILLNESS IN THE STORM

wo weeks after the 2005 General Synod of the United Church of Christ voted to approve a resolution supporting marriage equality, chaos reigned in novice clergywoman Karen's Pennsylvania congregation. Following attendance at her first General Synod, Karen chose to take a week's vacation at the beach. Refreshed, relaxed, and still inspired in the afterglow of her first General Synod, she was unprepared for the knock on her study door the Monday following her return. Kevin, the usually genial and upbeat president of the consistory, or church governing council, somberly described what had been going on in the congregation since news of the resolution had become known. "Pastor, I'm worried. I'm not taking sides, but at least a third of the consistory want to vote to leave the denomination. I've gotten calls asking where you stand on this issue and what you're going to do about it when you get back from vacation."

Karen's sense of refreshment evaporated in a few short moments. She could feel the tension of the "fight or flight response" rising in her neck and between her shoulder blades. Although she had worked hard to be the spiritual leader of this central Pennsylvania congregation in her first few months following graduation from seminary, for a moment she wished she'd said "yes" to the pulpit committee that had interviewed her for an associate minister's position in a large suburban congregation. "At least," she pondered, "I would be in the background, and I could safely let the senior pastor sweat this one out!"

As the consistory chair continued his litany of gloom, doom, and conflict, Karen was tempted to interject her own opinion. But something inspired her to "pause, take a few deep breaths, and simply listen to what he had to say." When she finally responded to his concerns, Karen thanked Kevin as she mirrored his sense of the gravity of the situation. Without raising her voice, she reminded him that the resolution's passage was nonbinding and that the congregational polity of the United Church of Christ allowed the congregation to decide its own policy about celebrating same-gender unions in the sanctuary. She suggested that they meet again in twenty-four hours to come up with a response to the issue at hand.

When Kevin left, Karen decided that she could not respond to the impending crisis on her own. First, she conferred with her conference minister and then contacted Bruce, who had just been on the phone with two other recently ordained pastors facing similar congregational crises because of the controversial Synod resolution. Then, after she read the mail that had accumulated in her absence, she took a brisk walk around her community, praying and asking for God's guidance.

In a matter of days, Bruce organized a "round table" to support and provide counsel on this situation to newly ordained pastors in Lancaster Theological Seminary's Wholeness in Ministry program. The goal of this gathering was not to support a particular position on the issue of marriage equality, but to help pastors deal creatively, professionally, and spiritually with the potential congregational conflict raised by the resolution. As Karen prayed and shared with other pastors facing the same challenges, she experienced a greater sense of confidence that, with God's help and a small group of dedicated leaders, she and her congregation could weather the storm.

Drawing on the wisdom of Edwin Friedman's congregational systems theory, over the next few months, Karen sought to be a "nonanxious presence" in her congregation. Although she clearly expressed her own theologically moderate position and her loyalty to the United Church of Christ, she also made it clear that her ultimate goal was to enable the congregation to remain faithful to God's leading in the context of its historic relationship with the German Reformed and United Church of Christ traditions. "Many nights I had trouble sleeping. I worried that the church might vote to leave the denomination, and if that happened, I would have to resign. I loved these people, but I was ordained in the United Church of Christ and would remain loyal to the church of my childhood even though I was not prepared to perform same-gender marriages." As she looks back on that contentious period, Karen acknowledges the importance of her faith in God's presence guiding and protecting her, keeping her centered despite her anxiety. "Instead of panicking, I remembered to 'pray my fears.' Every time I felt my anxiety rising in a consistory meeting, I closed my eyes, took a deep breath, and asked for wisdom. I paused before I spoke. Though I disagreed with the positions taken by the more conservative members of the church, I knew that they were acting in good faith. They were operating out of their understanding of scripture and the social norms of central Pennsylvania culture. In fact, I used the crisis as an opportunity to get to know some of them better! Nothing would be accomplished by demonizing them or belittling their theological stance. Instead, I organized a Bible study on sexuality and biblical interpretation, not just the issues of homosexuality. There was no consensus, but people heard one another and came to appreciate the diversity of our congregation."

Today, Karen's congregation remains active in the United Church of Christ. While many members still disagree with the liberal wing of the denomination, their pledges to the conference and the church's general ministry have remained stable. Karen attributes her own survival during this time of crisis to taking time to listen for God's guidance, which enabled her to step back, calm her panic response, find a spiritual center, and reach out to mentors and colleagues for counsel. "I couldn't have made it alone," Karen admits, "I needed to listen to God's still small voice speaking in my heart and in the wisdom of my seminary mentor and pastoral colleagues.

TRANSFORMING CONFLICT

Conflict is an essential aspect of life. The biblical tradition is filled with conflict situations in families, national, and religious life, many of which end in division or murder. In fact, the Bible presents us with many graphic images of dysfunctional family relationships and prophet-killing communities. It may be that the contentious communities in Corinth and Galatia are more typical of congregational experience than many of us would like to admit! Issues of theology, hospitality, economics, gender, sexuality, and leadership style still threaten to divide congregations today.

It is inevitable that healthy transformational and visionary leadership will lead to a certain level of congregational resistance and conflict. According to Chris Hobgood, resistance "can be defined as energy that rises up to counter change in a system."[1] Hobgood also notes that the presence of resistance can be a "sign of vital, high-quality, and faithful life in a congregation."[2] Vital, renewed, and renewing ministries can expect that congregational growth and renewed vision will always challenge the "way things are" and may even force change agents out of their comfort zones. Change contributes to stress, whether in our bodies or in congregational life. Healthy, dynamic pastors need to know how creatively to transform conflict and resistance!

According to systems theory, congregational systems, like families, tend to seek levels of stability or homeostasis, appropriate to their self-understanding, sense of threat, and previous family of origin or congregational experiences. When congregational patterns of behavior change too quickly or new visions for the future arise, even if these new initiatives will ultimately benefit the church and enable it to fulfill its mission more creatively, some members of the congregation will cling to the status quo and challenge the authority of anyone who would inject alternative possibilities into what they perceive as a stable system.[3]

No matter how hard they try, many persons simply cannot integrate change and growth at the pace it is occurring in their communities and congregations. Instead of initiating novelty to match environmental change, they hold on to the security of the past. In so doing, they tend to numb out, drop out, deny the change, or fight it for all they're worth. Few of us, including those of us committed to creative transformation, can immediately leap into initiating novelty to match the changes of our environment. Except in emergency situations, pastoral leaders also need a moment to pause and reflect, get their bearings, and find their spiritual center before imagining and implementing new possibilities.

As you consider healthy images of responding to congregational conflict, how do you deal with rapid change in your life and the church? Do you find yourself initially uncomfortable or defensive? Do you find yourself held "captive" to certain knee-jerk reactions?

Resistance happens in the best of ministries. We believe that the way pastors respond to healthy, or dysfunctional, resistance within their congregations reflects their spiritual and emotional maturity, leadership and relational skills, and sense of vision. Some pastors are tempted to react to resistance through argumentativeness, defensiveness, and promoting stereotypes of the opposition that polarize already contentious situations. While clear and wisely considered direct confrontation may be necessary in times of transformation, ministerial confrontation should always be guided by an awareness of God's vision for the congregation's future in terms of shalom, peace, healing, and wholeness for all, rather than reactive individual win-lose power dynamics. In the spirit of Paul's image of the "mind of Christ" (Phil. 2:5–11), pastors are challenged to use their power in ways that promote reconciliation and healing in their congregations.

In a world of diverse theological viewpoints, lifestyles, and personality types, conflict is inevitable. Further, certain congregational conflicts may linger for generations as a result of past pastoral misconduct, the intrusive presence of former pastors in the neighborhood, past or current intentional or unintentional inappropriate boundary violations by laypersons, or previous congregational theological divisions. We believe that even during their "honeymoon" periods, pastors should begin to draw nurture and support from mentors, colleagues, and spiritual directors in order to respond to conflict and resistance creatively.

Conflict, like the passage of time, can never be fully resolved or managed, but we can learn professional skills and spiritual practices that will enable us to experience stillness amid the storm. Though we might wish to fight, flee, or freeze, deep down we know that conflict in our congregations is healthy and must be addressed in order for pastors and congregations to experience the vitality, vision, and healing that God seeks for them. If we are to find wholeness and vitality for our congregations and ourselves in conflict situations, we must join professional expertise, knowledge of congregational systems, and a deep and humble awareness of God's sustaining, inspiring, and reconciling presence.

Our response to conflict is ultimately a spiritual issue, reflecting our theology, spiritual practices, and commitment to embrace God's "ministry of reconciliation" (2 Cor. 5:17) as we seek to balance transformative leadership with pastoral care. As overwhelming as conflict may seem and as threatened as the pastor may feel at times, we are called to affirm that God's creative and life-transforming vision will outlast any conflict and fears we might have. Like Christ's transformation of our lives, effective transformation of conflict is not ultimately of our own doing, but humbly received as a gift from God.[4] God's aim at justice, vitality, and beauty in the lives of persons and communities will always be unsettling to the status quo and our own visions of the future. Creative transformation, whether in our personal lives, in the nonhuman world, or in institutions, always involves a degree of change and destruction; but God is with us and also our opponents, seeking to heal the pain and alienation and providing alternative possibilities for human understanding and compassion. Openness to God's vision of reconciliation "transforms the moral character of individual disputants and eventually society as a whole."[5] How pastors spiritually frame and respond to conflict and resistance may lead to burnout and inappropriate behavior or to vitality and creativity.

FINDING STILLNESS IN THE STORM

The synoptic gospels tell the story of the disciples' response to a storm at sea. As they crossed the Sea of Galilee, the disciples were caught off guard by a fierce windstorm. As the wind howled and the waves beat against their boat, they panicked until they remembered that Jesus was with them, quietly sleeping in the back of the boat.

When the disciples called out to Jesus, "Lord save us! We are perishing!" (Matt. 8:25), Jesus awakened and calmed their hearts and the threatening storm, and then challenged them with the questions, "Why are you afraid? Have you no faith?"

As we read the story, we suspect that the narrative portrays two miracles, only one of which involved calming the actual storm. The first "miracle" involved the disciples' pausing long enough to remember that they were ultimately safe because Jesus was with them amid the storm. At that moment of relational and theological inspiration, their fear began to subside and their faith in God's protective presence was renewed. They saw the storm in the wider perspective of Jesus' presence and power. Despite the threatening storm, Jesus would not let them drown.

As we reflect on the gospel story, we imagine that the storm continued for a period of time after the disciples awakened Jesus. But, now, the disciples remained calm and returned to the task of guiding their boat through the storm, as God's peace descended upon the lake and their spirits. The second "miracle" was the eventual calming of the wind and the waves. We imagine that their newly found awareness of God's nearness inspired them to take action to save the boat and to claim their role as Jesus' partners in ministry, with or without the external calming of the sea.

The disciples found peace amid the storm through theological insight, "Jesus the savior and teacher is here with us and will protect us." Like Jesus' disciples, we discover that lived theology, relational support, and spiritual practice as well as sound leadership theory and skills are, accordingly, our primary ways to experience calm, courage, and confidence amid the storms of ministry. Awakening to God's still, small voice in the storm provides us with a quiet center from which to embrace, in a reconciling manner, diversity of opinion as well as inevitable change.

PRACTICING THEOLOGY IN CHALLENGING SITUATIONS

Vital and holistic theology joins vision and practice to transform conflict, resistance, and crisis in our congregations. We believe that becoming a nonanxious presence is more a matter of spiritual stature and theological insight than leadership training. When Susan heard the rumors that a small group within the congregation would seek her resignation as a result of her visionary leadership in opening the congregation to the changing neighborhood, including a growing population of Hispanic, African American, and gay, lesbian, bisexual, and transgender persons, she was initially shocked and wanted to crush the rebellion quickly and decisively. But, as she observed her initial response, she realized that it was similar in spirit to that of the group that opposed her leadership. "I thought I was practicing hospitality and inclusion, but I realized that I had my own set of 'outcasts,' mostly those who wanted to hang on to the church's homogenous glory days and sit in their pews, comfortably surrounded by folks like themselves. I had forgotten one of my key theological affirmations, my belief in the presence of God's light in every person, even those from whom I felt polarized. I realized that if I were to be true to my beliefs, I would have to see God's light in the old timers who wanted to get rid of me."

Susan responded to the minority faction pastorally, administratively, and spiritually. She realized that she could not deny the threat to her position, but she also knew that the majority of the congregation, including the church board, had supported the vision of hospitality, openness, and community involvement. Accordingly, she did not respond immediately to the resistance within her congregation. Like the disciples during the storm at sea, she remembered that Christ would be with her in the conflict and that Christ would have the final word in her ministry and congregation. "Instead of acting quickly, I made an appointment with my spiritual director. I needed the perspective that comes from prayer and stillness." Instead of succumbing to the temptation to respond immediately, Susan also chose to take a weekend at the beach, where she could walk, pray, and visualize the healing of congregation, including her opponents as well as supporters.

Susan also sought out the guidance of a trusted mentor from her seminary who was experienced in congregational systems theory and healthy conflict transformation. Following a lengthy conversation with her mentor, she decided to bring the issue to the church board without judgment or criticism, but as an important aspect of the inclusive vision that her congregation had adopted. Susan wanted to be sure that the congregation's leaders were aware of the resistance within the congregation and that they were willing to stand by congregation's agreed upon vision of the future, despite the potential "costs" of this discipleship. She clearly defined her own vision, and the vision the congregation had affirmed, while making a commitment to be a pastor to *all* persons in her congregation, regardless of their position on the church's new outreach to the community.

During this time of potential divisiveness, Susan also chose to contact directly the persons who had been the primary critics of her leadership and the congregation's new direction. She realized that they were also acting on good faith. They believed that the changes that were being implemented would threaten the religious community that had nurtured and sustained them for decades. Susan did not seek to convince them of the rightness of her position, but to enter into a sensitive and creative pastoral and theological dialogue. "I realized that their pastoral needs were as weighty as those of the surrounding community. I apologized for any pain or discomfort that they might be feeling, but reiterated the importance of the congregation's vision of hospitality."

Susan chose to embody the principle of healthy self-differentiation by holding clearly to her vision while remaining pastorally warm and available to those who questioned that vision. While many of the dissenting group stood their ground, only a few left the congregation.

Today the congregation, including those who initially opposed the new congregational outreach, is united behind their vital outreach to the whole community. While the congregation still has a long way to go in becoming a truly "rainbow" community, its Sunday attendance is beginning to reflect the ethnic, socioeconomic, and sexual diversity of the community in which it is located.

Many members of the dissenting group were persons who had spent decades working in the church's traditional mission and education programs. As a result of her willingness to embrace their concerns while maintaining her spiritual vision, many of these same people now indirectly support the church's new mission by bringing casseroles for the weekly community dinner and preparing coffee and donuts for the GLBT parents' support group.

As she looks back on that time of resistance, Susan recalls, "I had a few sleepless nights. I wanted to succeed and be loved, but I knew I had to be faithful to God's vision as I understood it. My salvation during this time of resistance was prayer, collegial professional mentoring, spiritual support from my director, and my pastoral compassion, yoked with my desire to hold to the inclusive vision mandated by my conscience."

VISIONARY LEADERSHIP IN UNSETTLING TIMES

"Be still and know that I am God" (Psa. 46:10) is still good counsel to progressive and mainstream spiritual leaders today. While the once dominant mainline Christianity has been relegated to the sidelines of America's spiritual landscape, eclipsed by increased secularization of our culture, on the one hand, and by aggressive fundamentalist and evangelical outreach programs and their accompanying "pop culture" of Christian music, books, and kitchen kitsch, on the other, new "battle lines" are being drawn by conservative Christian politicians in a way that threatens the separation of church and state.

In describing this "perfect storm" that has hit mainstream Christianity, Richard Hamm, who served as general minister and president of the Christian Church (Disciples of Christ) from 1993 to 2000, notes the collision of several factors in the last twenty years: the dramatic shift in culture from the modern to postmodern era, the increasingly obsolete organizational structures inherited from the modern era, and the fear that has turned mainstream Christianity inward from mission to maintenance and survival. In responding to the cultural and spiritual storms of our time, Hamm counsels that we must examine our theological, cultural, and organizational assumptions.[6]

As we consider the challenges spiritual leaders face in our time, we are reminded of the upheavals described in Psalm 46. We imagine that these words were first heard by the beleaguered spiritual leadership of Israel. Perhaps the leaders of Israel, like many of today's pastors, had once assumed stability and growth in their national and economic lives. But, with little warning, they found themselves plunged into a season of spiritual and political disorientation where everything was up for grabs and a return to normalcy a phantasm. Listen to these descriptions of the world as if they were spoken to you in the context of your congregation, community, and denomination:

> the earth is changing . . .
> the mountains are shaking in the heart of the sea. . .
> the waters are roaring and foaming . . .
> the mountains trembling with its tumult . . .

Do these phrases describe the setting in which your ministry, congregation, or denomination finds itself as it interacts with the postmodern, technologically savvy, spiritually pluralistic, yet religiously uncertain world?

Although we have focused on the importance of a pastor's spiritual life and personal health and vitality in fostering transformative congregational ministry, we also recognize that pastoral leaders must learn "big picture" navigational skills in order to flourish in the midst of our rapidly changing world in which the structures, including denominational, cultural, and ecological structures, that we once depended upon are now at risk. Today's leaders, like those who first chanted Psalm 46, must be agile generalists, able to shift from local politics to global concerns, theological reflection to church administration, pastoral care to community advocacy, preaching preparation to family crises, in the space of just a few hours.

Like most of us, surrounded by upheaval, the psalmist was, no doubt, tempted to run for cover and to succumb to the survival patterns of the reptilian brain—fight, flight, or freeze. Upheaval appeared to be winning the day. Jerusalem's leaders were frightened and circling the wagons, hoping simply to survive the onslaught. But within and beyond the struggles of the day and the worries of the future, the psalmist found comfort and energy from the faithfulness of God, which gave him a sense of quiet amid the storm. The psalmist, like spiritual leaders in our time, discovered that divine fidelity, vision, and energy were his only hope amid the perfect storm. The psalmist's words are still a great comfort to us in ministry today:

> God is our refuge and strength,
>> a very present help in trouble.
> Therefore we will not fear, though the earth should change,
>> though the mountains shake in the heart of the sea; . . .
> God is in the midst of the city; it shall not be moved;
> God will help it when the morning dawns. . . .
> Be still, and know that I am God! (Psa. 46:1–2,5, 10a)

As Walter Brueggemann notes in his commentaries on the Psalms, the dynamic spiritual journey involves the dynamic interplay of orientation and stability; disorientation, loss, and grief; and new orientation—the emergence of a new, just, and spiritually vital order.[7] Today's spiritual leaders must expect to navigate the seas of disorientation, trusting—without any guarantees—that a new orientation is on the horizon. Quiet companionship with our faithful God places our panic and hopelessness in a larger perspective. From this larger perspective, we can integrate the stability necessary for institutional survival with the agility essential for transformation and growth.

In times of upheaval, leaders must maintain a dynamic and flexible vision, find ways to ground the vision in the concrete setting in which they minister, and provide guidance and energy to inspire lay leaders to embody an even larger vision than the pastor's own vision for the transformation, healing, and empowering of congregations and denominations. Vital leadership in the postmodern era must be large enough to embrace the many-faceted world and lively enough to adapt to the constant communal, technological, global, and institutional change that will emerge in the decade ahead.

Jesus grew in "wisdom and stature" and so must today's spiritual leaders. How do you attend to the ordinary moments of everyday ministry, while yet still entertaining visions of hope for your congregation's and community's future? What daily practices do you need to hold together the many diverse images and viewpoints in the context of a centered, but dynamic and flexible vision of ministry?

Leadership in the context of the perfect storm of mainstream Christianity is relational and spiritual. As you shift sails with the whipping winds, you must, like the South African Sankofa bird, look backward in order to stay in touch with tradition and those for whom the past is a treasure to be preserved and, at the same time, look ahead expecting and planning to see God's next creation.

To maintain the vision that embraces the past and imagines the future, weathers the storms of controversy and resistance, and stays in contact with allies and opponents alike, spiritual leaders need to remember to "be still" or "pause awhile" to experience God in their midst. Quiet openness and responsiveness to God's presence in the storm helps us find our quiet center and maintain our lively vision amid the chaotic waters of congregational resistance and transformation. In the quiet, we remember our vision and discover God's new visions for our ministry and community.

SPIRITUAL LEADERSHIP AND THE APPRECIATIVE WAY

Without a vision, a pastor cannot face the challenges of change and resistance. But if the pastor's vision is not creatively and honestly shared by her or his faith community, congregations will deny the need for change, turn on their pastoral and lay leadership, or fall into divisive conflict. Congregational change is the result of vital and visionary leadership that mirrors, reflects, inspires, and challenges the congregation's own creative imagination, rooted in the interplay of its "best and highest" practices of its past and its loftiest dreams for its future.

Recently, the practice of "appreciative inquiry" has surfaced as one pathway of professional and congregational transformation. Inspired by the social constructivist, organizational development work of David Cooperrider, appreciative inquiry focuses on solutions, rather than problems, in the quest for creative institutional transformation. Grounded in the theological vision of a creative, loving purpose always at work in the universe, appreciative inquiry is a lively tool for congregational visioning and strategic planning. In the spirit of the Sankofa bird, appreciative inquiry asserts that growth comes through building our visions of the future on the core values, words, and images gleaned from our congregation's most inspiring and fulfilling achievements of the past.

Creative congregational change also responds gracefully to resistance. Rather than opposing those who resist the call of the future, appreciative inquiry first asks in subtle and indirect ways, "Why are you afraid of change?" and "What do you need to feel safe in a changing world?" The appreciative way honors the gifts and traditions of those who are attached to "the way things were" in a changing congregational setting by inviting those who resist change to remember what was most life-giving about the past that can be utilized in shaping the future of the congregation.

Vital and visionary pastoral leadership affirms the value of past achievements as the basis of faithful transformation in the future. Guided by her or his vision of the future, the pastor invites the congregation to collectively and prayerfully articulate a dream for the future and then begin to formulate the steps needed to achieve that future toward which God is calling them.

Unlike problem-oriented approaches, the appreciative way experiences divine inspiration in all persons, including those who resist change. By lis-

tening to these persons' visions of an ideal earlier era and their hope for congregational stability in the future, the appreciative inquiry approach invites
those who resist the call of the future to articulate complementary visions
of the future that can contribute to the congregation's emerging vision.

Visionary leadership practices what it preaches. It initiates novelty to
match the novelty of the environment, including the pastor's own life. The
visionary pastor lives in a world of multiple possibilities. The strength of his
or her congregational vision is undergirded by lively visions for his or her
family life, personal growth, spiritual formation, and professional excellence. Joining the far horizon with the next step on the journey, such visionary leaders are attentive to persons and details as well as to God's great
dream for her or his congregation. He or she faces congregational resistance
and conflict with flexibility and endurance, grounded in the confidence
that God's vision draws all of us, some expectantly and others reluctantly,
toward a future of beauty, justice, and truth.[8] The ability to maintain a positive vision of the future amid congregational resistance and conflict feeds
the fire of pastoral transformation and enables pastors to remain vital, renewed, and renewing in their professional and relational lives.

FEEDING THE MINISTERIAL FIRE

Healthy pastoral leadership joins self-awareness, spiritual centeredness,
good communication skills, and the ability to imagine and share God's vision for the future of your congregation. Good leaders do their own inner
work as they practice the art of mindfulness in ministry, recognizing their
own patterns of response in stressful situations and discovering ways to approach challenges in terms of the present moment rather than in terms
of knee-jerk responses based on past professional or family of origin experiences.

A Holistic Spiritual Practice

Like the disciples of the first century, today's pastors are easily tempted to
panic and forget God's presence in times of conflict and challenge. On your
own, without spiritual or relational resources, you may feel as if the storms
of ministry are overwhelming you. As an antidote, we invite you to experience the following exercise, which comes from our work with both recently

ordained and experienced pastors in Lancaster Theological Seminary ministerial excellence and wholeness programs.

Find a quiet and comfortable place where you can spend fifteen to twenty minutes in prayer. Begin simply by being still in God's presence, deeply and quietly breathing in God's shalom and protection in your life. Take time to read the story of "the storm at sea" from Mark 1:35–40 at least twice. What words and images leap out of the text and into your life? Pause and notice the wisdom for your life situation that you are receiving from God's voice within the text today.

Now, close your eyes and relax and image yourself caught in a "perfect storm." You may imagine yourself walking along the seashore or in a boat. Visually, what is it like to be engulfed by waves and wind? How do you feel when you are in the "center of a storm"—physically, spiritually, and emotionally?

As you look at your ministry, visualize metaphorically the "wind" and the "waves" that buffet you right now. What are the challenges that threaten your peace of mind and sense of security in ministry? Take a moment to visualize these challenges in more detail and your current response to them.

As you ponder the challenges and responses of your ministry, remind yourself that Jesus is with you and that he will not let you be swept away by the wind and waves. Visualize Jesus as with you in the storm. How does it feel to know that Jesus is your companion in the storm? Take time to share with Jesus your deepest needs. Ask him to be with you, and protect and guide you through the storm. What guidance is Jesus giving you amid the storm?

Visualizing Jesus as your companion, take a few moments to let yourself experience God's safety, protection, and guidance. Imagine Jesus guiding you and giving the strength to make it to the "far shore" of God's vision for your congregation. Whenever you find yourself being buffeted by the storms of ministry, remember that Jesus is with you.

A Practice for Healthy Ministry

Congregational systems theory affirms the relationship between the way church leaders respond to their family of origin and their current leadership and professional responses. Mindful ministry is grounded in the recognition that we are historical, relational, and dynamic beings, whose responses to conflict and change are first shaped, though not ultimately limited, by our family of origin.

Healthy pastors see the unfolding of our lives as a "holy adventure," reflecting the dynamic interplay of past, present, and future in each moment of decision. They see their past as potentially liberating rather than limiting. They recognize that each relationship can be a healing adventure if we see our encounters, even with those persons who "push our buttons," as an invitation to self-awareness and personal transformation.

Edwin Friedman and Ronald Richardson invite us to chart our family of origin, noting places of health and disease, distance and enmeshment, alienation and healing.[9] Charting a genogram, or map of our multigenerational family relationships, enables us to see our role in our families of origin and, then, to make connections between our current behaviors in congregational or family life and patterns of behavior we learned from our family system. Our goal in tracing our family relational heritage is not to blame our parents or grandparents but to become conscious of our habitual relational responses, both positive and negative, to certain situations in our personal and professional lives. When we discover and creatively engage our own or others' dysfunctional relational behaviors, we can gain freedom *from* habitual responses and freedom *for* personal and relational transformation.[10]

In reflecting on his own family of origin, Bruce discovered that when he is under stress he continues to reach out to others, doing all the right things, but becomes emotionally disengaged. Early in life, he learned that the only way to survive in his turbulent family was to go about his own business responsibly even though he had emotionally withdrawn from the persons involved. As a child, he could not fully embrace his family's pain and conflict. Today, he is still works at staying emotionally involved, rather than emotionally withdrawing during times of conflict and stress.

During her first congregational call, Susan realized that her mission in her family of origin was "to make everybody happy." "If my parents were happy," she confessed, "I thought they wouldn't fight or yell at me." Susan discovered that she was repeating the same behaviors in her relationship with influential persons in her congregation. "I would do anything to placate angry church members and avoid conflict. I constantly tried to respond to the needs of every disgruntled parishioner until I realized that I was losing myself in the process."

When she realized that she didn't have to repeat old childhood behaviors in her new setting, Susan found her own voice in ministry. "I still work for peace in the congregation. But now I'm not afraid of stating my viewpoint. When I know people will disagree, sometimes I catch myself apologizing for standing out in the crowd; but then I realize that they called me to be a spiritual leader to do just that. If I'm going to be faithful to my call, I need to stand on my own from time to time." Susan has learned that because God is with her, she doesn't need to fear conflict. God will provide resources and possibilities to respond creatively to conflicts that once terrified her.

The "family systems" genogram, studied with a spiritual coach or therapist, can be a tool for spiritual transformation and professional excellence. During her ten years as pastor of Washington, D.C., congregation, Kate found it very helpful to be in a colleague group, led by a family systems therapist, in which each participant completed a genogram and referenced it as they rotated presenting a case study from their congregation. The insights she received in the group helped her respond more creatively to issues of conflict and resistance in her congregation.

In finding freedom from the limitations of the past, we can become new and vital leaders in the present moment. Awareness of family systems, like understanding personality types, enables us to be more sympathetic to "difficult" persons in our congregations. Family systems theory helps us remember that beneath the façade of anger or triangulating behavior of these "difficult" persons there hides a beloved child of God whose behavior is really a cry for love, and our response is too! Our own personal healing and understanding of others takes us beyond habitual responses and knee-jerk defensiveness to lively, creative, and visionary leadership and action.

An Affirmation of Faith

Your ability to respond creatively to the storms of congregational and denominational ministry depends on your spiritual centeredness. Affirmations can free you from the limitations of the past in order to be open to the freedom of the future. In times of conflict, using affirmations is a reminder that God is your deep spiritual center, "[y]our refuge and strength, a very present help in trouble" (Psa. 46:1). We suggest the following affirmations as an antidote to defensiveness and anxiety during times of conflict.

- Nothing can separate me from the love of God.

- Congregational conflict cannot separate me from the love of God.

- In Christ, I am a new creation. I respond to the past in creative and healing ways.

- God gives me courage and peace amid the storm.

A Covenant of Wholeness and Vitality in Ministry

Responding creatively to change is a matter of choice and intentionality. Healthy and vital pastors choose to practice visionary leadership by committing themselves to professional and spiritual growth. As Sharon Daloz Parks notes, "Leadership can be taught."[11] It can also be learned through a commitment to life-transforming practices in the context of a creative, insightful, and supportive community. Visionary leadership emerges when we covenant to live our lives in the spirit of appreciative inquiry, looking at life in terms of abundance and growth, rather than scarcity and security. Living by the following covenants can transform your ministry and personal life.

- I covenant to look at my life in terms of solutions rather than problems.

- I covenant to explore my life history with gratitude, opening to God's healing of my past, present, and future.

- I covenant to look for God's presence in persons with whom I am in conflict.

EIGHT

CELEBRATING YOURSELF IN MINISTRY

The philosopher Socrates once noted that wisdom is to be found in following the simple words "know thyself." Vital, transformative, spiritually centered, and healthy ministry over the long haul is, in good measure, the gift of hard-earned self-awareness in the context of your ministerial and relational setting. While we cannot fully control the behavior of our congregations or manage the hours of our day, a commitment to living with mindfulness in terms of our gifts, responses, and priorities enables us to feed the ministerial fire daily and over a lifetime of ministry. As we have affirmed throughout this book, pastoral self-awareness, embodied in a commitment to continuing theological and professional education, spiritual formation, healthy relationships, and self-care, is the primary means of preventing ministerial burnout.

Today there are a variety of temperament and personality type preference instruments for giving insight on one's gifts, abilities, and areas of growth, such as the Enneagram, the Kiersey Bates Temperament Test, and the Myers Briggs Personality Type Indicator (MBTI). Grounded in the psychological wisdom of Carl Jung, the MBTI enables pastors to understand their unique gifts for ministry and also appreciate the diverse gifts of persons with different personalities within their families and congregations. In this chapter, our goal will be to present a broad outline of personality types and their relationship to practicing healthy and vital ministry. Accordingly, we will not attempt to give a comprehensive description of personality types described by the MBTI, but will describe how a pastor's awareness of her or his personality type can become a catalytic factor in healthy, vital, and successful ministry. We believe that awareness of our gifts and limitations due to our personality types as well as openness to growing in personal stature by honoring and embracing the gifts of other personality types in our congregations enables pastors to shine forth, rather than burn out, in their ministerial and personal lives.[1] We also recognize that identifying our personality type or the personality types of others is the beginning, rather than the end, of our journey toward vital self-awareness that Carl Jung calls "individuation." Individuation is a process that takes a lifetime. We are always "larger" than our personality type, which is intended to be an opening to discovery rather than a box within which to imprison ourselves or others. If we make a commitment to self-awareness, over a lifetime our personality type will evolve in relationship to our experiences, spiritual practices, and personal and professional growth.

DIFFERENCE IS BEAUTIFUL

John's gospel proclaims that the light that enlightens everyone has come into the world (John 1:9). Divine beauty shines through every life, joining nature and nurture, and call and response, in the holy adventure of self-discovery and vocational transformation. The Apostle Paul reflects this same dynamic in his affirmation that there are many gifts, all of which flourish in relationship to one another, arising from the creativity of one Spirit within the lively and interdependent body of Christ (1 Cor. 12:4–31). Delighting in the gifts of others in the body of Christ and their value to the wider faith community, we are invited to celebrate our own unique experience of God's wisdom revealed in our truest, deepest self and, at the same time, celebrate the gifts of others. We hope that as you listen to the unique approaches to life embodied in our own professional and personal stories as well as in the stories of others in this chapter, you will be awakened to your own lively personality gifts for ministry.

Introverted by nature, Bruce, an MBTI "I" type, finds his greatest energy and personal renewal in the solitude of writing, walking, contemplation, and study. His day begins before sunrise with prayer and meditation, a solitary walk through our Lancaster neighborhood, and then an hour of reading or writing before Kate rises. As a seminary administrator, professor, entrepreneur, and local church pastor who often spends his days representing seminary programs, teaching, or meeting with colleague groups, Bruce surprises his colleagues and friends when he admits that he is introverted by nature. Although extraverted in his professional life, especially in terms of his integration of heart and mind, feeling and thinking, Bruce needs a few hours each day for study and contemplation in order to stay balanced and lively in his professional and family life. Happily, Kate is not an early riser, for when she wakes up she likes to share her dreams during the night and plans for the day with Bruce!

When he was a new pastor, Bruce often came home exhausted from church on Sunday afternoons and took a long nap simply to recover from the ardors of extroverted interpersonal encounters and pubic speaking required by the rigors of Sunday pastoral duties. Although Bruce's personal journey has led to a creative integration of introversion and extroversion, so that he is now seldom drained by several hours of intense public activity, he still takes time each day, and especially during demanding professional and personal times, for disciplined times of prayer and meditation. Even a few minutes with a theological text or spiritual practice revives Bruce for the next personal or professional adventure. As a MBTI "J" or judging type, Bruce finds it quite easy to practice spiritual disciplines, write, and exercise on a regular basis. Like the tortoise in Aesop's fable, Bruce works consistently, applying himself to the tasks at hand one day at a time, with regularity and discipline. He usually not only meets deadlines, but exceeds them. He often writes sermons and lectures several weeks in advance.

Kate's strongly extroverted MBTI "E" type and ambient "perceiving" or "P" type personality complements Bruce's more introverted and disciplined approach to life. Kate finds energy in spontaneous activities and multiple friendships, and the more the merrier. A day of good pastoral conversation, leading workshops, or worship services leaves Kate eager for further conversations and encounters. Kate is always up for going out for a meal or dessert with congregants following worship. Although Kate has come to integrate more introverted spiritual disciplines into her personal and professional life, she remains most renewed by spiritual practices undertaken in groups and that involve motion or sound such as body prayer, yoga, and chanting. Although she has always been in one-on-one spiritual direction, she is most nourished by the synergy of group spiritual retreats and interactive worship. She works tirelessly to nurture the lively, relational, and spontaneous worship of our "emerging" progressive congregation. As a MBTI "P" or perceiving type, Kate joins long-term vision with the spontaneity of the moment. She usually pushes deadlines and prefers her workday to "flow" along without being too tightly planned. Like the hare in Aesop's fable, Kate always finishes the race, but her route is often characterized by starts and stops, sprinting and resting, and excursions along the back roads. Recently, in order to deepen her contemplative, more introverted side, Kate enrolled in a two-year spiritual formation and direction training program, sponsored by the Oasis Ministries for Spiritual Development.[2]

Over thirty years of marriage, we have learned how to work together in ways that bring greater energy, warmth, and creativity to our personal and professional lives. During our early years together, however, our differences were often a source of conflict and judgment. We are fortunate that we both share being intuitive, feeling type personalities (MBTI "NF" types). This means that we both take in information primarily by indirect, intuitive means and that we make decisions based primarily on feeling and value considerations. Although our differing personalities lead to very different problem-solving approaches, we have learned, and are still learning, to appreciate our differences within the context of our frequent teamwork. Further, over three decades of personal and professional partnerships, Bruce has learned to let go of his need for immediate clarity in terms of process and planning, and Kate has learned to be more disciplined and regular in her spiritual life and professional planning. Kate is learning how to pause, be still, and listen for divine inspiration, while Bruce is learning to appreciate the value of more extroverted spiritual activities such as body prayer and group chanting. We have discovered that difference in personality type can lead to contrast and creativity rather than conflict and contention. We have learned that beauty and creativity in work and marriage are the gifts of complementary differences rather than homogenous uniformity.

MINISTERIAL TYPE

"In the body of Christ there are many personality types and gifts." The nature of our gifts and vocation within the Christian community is intimately related to our personality type. While we believe that each person's personality type is dynamic and evolving, depending on environment, maturity, and intentionality, our unique personality types profoundly influence the growth and health of our spiritual life, leadership style, and vocational orientation. The divine call and response comes in and through our personality type as well as our age, gender, sexual orientation, and life experiences. Accordingly, vitality in ministry is grounded in our openness to God's call within our own unique gifts and personality type. In the following sections, we will reflect on the role of personality type in creative and vital ministry.

As we reflect on our unique and diverse approaches to experiencing the universe, making decisions, being energized, and taking in information, we need to remember that the MBTI, according to Otto Kroeger and Roy Oswald, "does not measure intelligence nor focus on pathologies or deviation. The model is one of health and wholeness."[3] In the spirit of Meister Eckhardt's affirmation that "all things are words of God," difference in personality is a call to gratitude and wonder, and an invitation to growing in wisdom and stature by embracing the holy otherness of different personality types as they are creatively embraced in your own life and in the lives of others. The sixteen possible personality configurations proposed by the MBTI typology find their basis in the interplay of four pairs of contrasting types that we will describe in terms of the relationship of personality type and healthy ministerial practices.

Energy and Eros: Introvert and Extrovert

Healthy ministry involves the constant transformation of the divine and human energy flowing through our lives. As spirit persons, pastors mediate the energy they receive in order to illumine, enlighten, and empower their congregations. Pastors who flourish in ministry recognize what enhances and depletes the flow of God's energy in their lives.

Introverted pastors, for example, experience the flow of divine energy into their lives through intentional times of solitude and quiet. While introverted pastors work as intensely as their extroverted companions in ministry, they need to set aside time and space for spiritual and relational energizing.

An introverted pastor, Susan, describes the challenges introverts face as they seek to maintain excellence and vitality in ministry. "Some days I go from meeting to meeting, responding to congregational business as well as the pastoral needs of members. By late afternoon, I'm totally spent. If I don't have a half an hour break by 3:00 P.M., I have trouble listening to those who come to seek my spiritual counsel. I am virtually brain dead if I have an evening meeting." In order to stay spiritually and professionally fresh and connected with her congregants, Susan has learned to take at least one afternoon each week for a miniretreat. "That afternoon retreat gives me the energy and perspective I need to maintain a sense of God's presence throughout the busy days and weeks of ministry." She also takes quarterly overnight retreats at a cabin near her home.

Extroverts, on the other hand, experience divine energy best when they are in relationship with others. Extroverted pastors thrive on busy relational days and often end a busy day, as Kate puts it, "panting for more," hoping to have one more conversation with a congregant. While introverts rejoice in quiet mornings and solitary retreats, extroverts need personal and external sources of inspiration in order feel fully attuned with God's presence in the world. Extroverts thrive on action. They also have a strong sense of "spirituality of place and people." Contemplation needs to be balanced or combined with action in order for extroverts to remain committed to a particular spiritual discipline.

An extroverted pastor, Natalie rejoices when her days are filled with appointments and meetings. "I feel most alive when I am part of the action, leading worship and programs." Now in her second call, Natalie recalls the pain she felt during her first congregational call to a two-hundred-member congregation in a town of three thousand people. "I loved the people. But I was bored by the lack of activity and personal contacts. I only had a part-time secretary and no one ever stopped by to visit during the week. To compound matters, I lived fifty miles from any town of consequence. As a single person, I had no one to talk with and nothing to do when I left the office. I almost went crazy." In order to find balance in her personal and professional life, initially Natalie became active in conference committees and enrolled in a doctor of ministry program at the local seminary. But still she needed more day-to-day contact in order to feel vital and centered. After three years, Natalie was called to a congregation in a larger, college town, where she finds energy and stimulation through regularly participating in cultural programs and religious and political interest groups. Natalie notes, "I have found my spiritual home here. Now I have plenty to do. I entertain regularly and go out to cultural programs nearly every week. I feel energized and happy to be involved in so many persons' lives."

Embracing Reality: Sensing and Intuition

Long before the dawn of postmodernism, it was clear that persons experience the world in vastly different ways. On the one hand, many persons focus on a factual approach to embracing reality. Whenever a friend or colleague waxes poetic, they bring them back to concrete realities of budgets, bricks, and mortar with their own version of TV detective Joe Friday's statement "just the facts, ma'am." This approach to life, described as *sensing* by the MBTI, is interested in the intricate details of life. From this perspective, you only really know something when you can measure, weigh, or describe it in concrete terms. On the other hand, some persons are more interested in the unseen stretches of the forest than the particular details of the trees in front of them. These persons, described as *intuitives* by the MBTI, embrace reality and gather information in large bites, treasuring nuance, pattern, possibility, and imagination. While persons who gather information through the five senses want to know the bottom line, intuitive, or "N" types, want to know what possibilities can emerge from the details of everyday life. Intuitives need sensates, and sensates need intuitives for healthy decision-making and teamwork.

A healthy example of the interplay of sensing and intuition is found in the gospel story of the loaves and fishes. The disciples accurately describe the facts of the situation—there is boy who has five loaves and two fishes—

and they accurately note that they cannot feed five thousand persons with the contents of the boy's lunch pail. While Jesus recognizes the limitations present in the situation, Jesus intuitively imagines God's infinite power in the universe and opens himself to resources that go beyond the obvious sensory data. In this story, the trees and the forest, the details and imagination, complement one another and the multitude is fed. If God is omnipresent, then God is present both in the concrete world of budgets, leaky roofs, and tax forms and in the uncharted realm of possibility that emerges in relationship to the concrete details of life.

The dynamic of sensing and intuition is often lived out in congregational decision making. Sensates, or "S" types, often see the pastor and other more intuitive thinkers as so "heavenly minded that they are of no earthly good," when they propose programs that go far beyond the perceived resources of the congregation. (This dynamic is often the case in congregational life, since, according to one study, 57 percent of pastors are intuitive while 76 percent of the population are sensate.[4]) Intuitive persons may respond to the limitations of concrete and fact-based thinking with the admonition, "You, of little faith, God will provide." Yet highly intuitive pastors need their sensate members. Healthy decision making embraces both the concreteness of sensation and the broad perspective of intuition as it discerns possibility within the concrete realities of congregational life. Intuitive persons inspire us to "launch out into the deep," imagining the future God imagines for our congregation, while sensing persons remind us to make sure that we've checked the life vests and purchased enough supplies for the adventure.

Processing Reality: Judging and Perceiving

A typical interchange between Bruce and Kate goes as follows. On a Saturday morning, with no appointments or commitments planned for the day, over coffee Bruce asks Kate, "So, what are your plans for the day?" Kate responds, "I don't have any idea. I just got up and won't know for a few hours." A *judging* type, according to the MBTI, Bruce enjoys structure and consistency. He makes daily and weekly lists and constantly revises them. In the course of writing this book, Bruce spent an hour each morning over several months, with the exception of Sundays, gathering materials, doing research, and writing the text. As a *perceiving* type, Kate, on the other hand, multitasks from dawn to dusk in what she calls an "amoebic" fashion. When ideas and thoughts come to her, she jots them down on notepaper jammed in her purse, shares them on the run with Bruce, and then takes breaks for them to germinate. Only when faced with "deadlines" does Kate apply herself to background research and committing her ideas to writing.

The same dynamic is at work in our sermon preparation. In our congregation, each of us typically preaches every other week. Bruce begins reflecting on the lectionary reading a day or so after he preaches his most recent sermon and works consistently throughout the week, usually completing his text at least a week before delivering his sermon. Kate, on the other hand, doesn't begin to percolate her thoughts till the beginning of the week in which she will preach and seldom begins writing her sermon until Friday.

The deep wisdom of Aesop's fable is that both the tortoise and the hare finish the race, but in very different ways. Judging types are self-disciplined, consistent, orderly, and decisive. It is important that judging types are not "judgmental," just organized and consistent. Perceiving types are flexible, agile, always seeking novelty, spontaneous, and open-ended. While "J" types want closure, "P" types like pushing boundaries, "seeking beyond" to imagine new possibilities. When a decision is made, "J"- types often want to move on to the next project, whereas "P" types are always open to revisiting previous decisions. As a "J-P" couple, our greatest challenge has been recreational and vacation planning. Together as a team, judging and perceiving leaders can bring life and zest to worship, relationships, and spiritual formation. Vitality in worship or everyday life is the gift of a creative blend of order and novelty, structure and chaos, predictability and spontaneity that arise from interplay of "J" and "P" approaches to reality. Indeed, the ministry of Jesus models a healthy blend of judging and perceiving. While Jesus honors the traditions of faith, he is willing to go beyond these traditions in novel ways in order to bring healing and wholeness to persons in need.

Divinity and Decision Making—Thinking and Feeling

Decision making eventually involves closure and taking one path rather than another. Every decision creates new possibilities, but also cuts off other possibilities. Even "P" types eventually come to the end of their "what ifs?" How we make decisions can be a source of conflict or companionship. *Thinking* types want to be objective as possible. Emphasizing logical and linear approaches to decision making, they want to exclude as much as possible the fuzziness of personality, subjectivity, and intuition. Decisions are best made when we have objective, clear-cut data, whether articulated through graphs, pie charts, statistics, or spread sheets. In congregational life, thinking types tend to make decisions based on the relationship between income and expenses, building utilization and expense—on cost-benefit analysis. When decisions have to be made that involve cuts in personnel or outreach to the neighborhood, thinking types rightly state, from their perspective, that "it's nothing personal." On the other hand, to *feeling* types, *everything* is personal and relational. In contrast to the quest for clarity typical of thinking types, feeling types make decisions in terms of values, emotions, relationships, and the unique emotional dynamics of those involved. Feelers need thinkers and thinkers need feelers!

The interplay of feeling and thinking can be seen in the medical field, where medical care has moved from a primary emphasis on objectivity to a growing concern for personal experience as a factor in health and illness. While medical doctors and nurses still take into consideration the more sensate world of research data and test data, they are coming to realize that statistics are always embodied in unique emotional, flesh and blood persons, which at times defy statistics and logic. Healthy decision making in the hospital or congregation involves an integration of objective and subjective, facts and faith, concreteness and possibility, and charts and compassion.

Creative Synthesis in Personality Types

While our study of personality types is meant to paint a picture of the MBTI in terms of ministerial life rather than a complete summary of personality type traits, one thing should be clear by now: each person lives out the gifts of his or her unique personality type in a dynamic, interdependent, and lively way. From these four sets of polarities, described as introvert-extrovert, intuitive-sensate, thinking-feeling, and judging-perceiving, emerge sixteen ever-changing constellations of personalities, each of which reflects the interplay of human potential, divine creativity, environmental influences, and personal decision making. The divine fire in its liveliness illuminates and energizes the prismatic nature of life, casting colorful patterns on the landscape of personal identity and family and congregational relationships. These constellations, or configurations, of personality type make for conflict, creativity, and wonder. Awareness of them shapes and guides our spiritual practices, work habits, and personal priorities.[5]

We believe that it is important to recognize that our personality types are not static forms, but rather dynamic and interdependent processes that can be influenced over a lifetime by nature and nurture. They evolve in terms of our faith, spiritual practices, choices, values, and life experiences. Indeed, the goal of life, as Jung says, is individuation or wholeness, which in the MBTI paradigm involves a dynamic and developing balance of the personality type polarities that enlivens and enriches our lives and the lives of those around us. In everyday life, personality types are fluid, and we move from one emphasis to another as we seek to respond creatively to challenges. After giving people their type scores and letters, we often hand out worksheets for developing an opposite preference. As they mature, introverts, whose natural inclination is contemplative, can learn to embrace the external liveliness of extroversion and, indeed, must include extroversion if they are to become effective in their public ministries. Maturely growing extroverts will eventually need to embrace the stillness of contemplative prayer, characteristic of introverts, if they are to balance depth with relationship in their preaching and pastoral care. Judging types will need to let go of their agendas in order to embrace the spontaneity of God's call that often disrupts our carefully scheduled days. Judging types need to learn to trust a deeper beauty and wisdom than what they could ever plan, a wisdom and beauty that will provide us with the necessary resources to preach and teach even when their preparation time is briefer than they desire. So too, perceiving types over time are called to welcome structure and order so that they can provide consistent and predictable pastoral leadership over the long haul. Sensing types will need to risk trusting God's storehouse of intuitive possibilities when they are tempted to cling to facts and sensate evidence as their source of security, while intuitives are challenged to ground their faith in the concrete realities of congregational statistics and resources.

Thinking types will need to awaken to considering the importance of values and relationships in gathering information along with their linear, logic-based decision-making, while feeling types must learn to engage more objective, linear thought processes along with their feeling-based passion to bring healing to vulnerable persons and provide adequate financial and logistic resources to respond to social injustice.

Without denying or neglecting our own personality gifts, our swiftly moving, postmodern world demands that we speed up the process of individuation that embraces the various polarities of life. In the journey of self-awareness, we are called to play with the "holy otherness" of our opposite types as we pursue the wholeness and healing that God envisages for us and the world. In the adventure of life, the most effective school for creative synthesis and personal wholeness is to be found in our willingness to examine our relationships and appreciate and learn from the uniqueness of others' approaches to reality. This holds true not just for personality type diversity but other social, racial, ethnic, sexual, and political diversities as well.

RELATIONAL TYPES

When she was called to be pastor of the Palisades Community Church in Washington, D.C., Kate asked the congregational leaders and as many laypersons as possible to take the self-scoring MBTI. Knowing that many challenges in personal and leadership relationships are the result of differences in personality type, Kate wanted to shape her ministry in accordance with the personality gifts of the congregation. While she was careful not to label people according to type in a fixed and literal way, her knowledge of the unique personalities in her congregation enabled her to work effectively with the church leadership, joining her gifts with their gifts, in order to promote faithful growth within the congregation.

When pastors and congregations are out of synch in terms of personality gifts and expectations, unnecessary conflicts can contribute to ministerial burnout. When he was called to the pastor of a large mid-Atlantic congregation, Ted was overjoyed. Little did he know that he would leave the congregation, disillusioned and burned out, in less than two years. Neither Ted nor his congregation saw the potential pitfalls of calling a contemplative, introverted, thinking type pastor to follow a wildly extroverted and feeling type pastor. Many congregants experienced Ted's more reserved and academic style as "cold" and "aloof," while Ted saw the more extroverted congregation as lacking spiritual depth. Although Ted worked long hours, making calls and leading meetings, he could never measure up to his entertaining, extroverted predecessor. Constantly trying to be something he wasn't eventually lead to exhaustion, and eventually to a medical crisis. After much reflection, Ted resigned the large congregation to accept a denominational position more suited to his contemplative, intellectual, and introverted spirit.

While "otherness" in terms of colleagues can be the source of frustration in pastoral administrative relationships, personality type differences can be synergetic when we creatively engage the holy otherness of God's presence in diverse personality types. As a MBTI perceiving type, Susan constantly frustrated her secretary by her last-minute approach to the bulletin and newsletter. Susan was also frustrated by her judging type secretary Patricia's constant reminding her about "deadlines" as if the "reign of God depended on it!" After months of mutual irritation, they took an afternoon away from the church to discuss their differing personality types. As they discussed their spiritual, family, and professional lives, they came to appreciate that their personality differences could be an asset rather than a debit in terms of administrative and pastoral effectiveness. With the help of Patricia, Susan created color-coded calendars, which she then went over on Mondays with Patricia, that reminded her when various congregational tasks were due. Patricia, on the other hand, learned that her constant nagging was not helpful. Instead, at their weekly meetings, she had the opportunity to remind Susan of all the important dates and make sure she noted them in her color-coded calendar. This gift of appreciation and awareness has led to an office that embraces both structure and spontaneity, laughter and professionalism.

The creative potential of personality types is reflected in the authors' teamwork as consultants, writers, and coministers. In many ways, despite our differences, we ideally complement one another. A solid INFJ, Bruce works consistently to birth new ideas, designing ways to embody these ideas in books and programs. After "writing down the bones" and "putting up the walls" of the text in solid "J" style, Bruce worked quietly on this book every morning before the family awakened, putting ideas to the test in the solitude of his own introverted experience. On the other hand, Kate, an ENFP, in good extroverted fashion developed her sections of the text orally in conversation with Bruce, who then took notes and incorporated them in the evolving structure of the book. In good "P" type fashion, Kate felt more comfortable expanding and "adorning" the text with anecdotal reflections and personal narratives than creating the linear structure that was second nature to Bruce. Because both of us are intuitive-feeling types, we enjoyed framing this text in terms of the experiences of pastors we had met and worked with, incorporating the lively theological categories of process-relational theology, expanding on the wisdom of professional experience, rather than being bound by adhering to abstract theological categories. As intuitive and feeling types, we do not find abstract theological categories appealing. Instead, we believe that theology is imaginative, evolving, relational, and open-ended rather than primarily linear. Wisdom is to be found in creative reflection on concrete and lively experience rather than abstract and unchanging theological categories. As a professor of practical and constructive theology, Bruce often surprises his students and colleagues by incorporating spiritual practices, pastoral narratives, music, art, and media in his classes and workshops.

This same dynamic inspires our creative partnership as consultants and copastors. Bruce quietly frames the curricula for workshops and sermons. After he finishes his broad outline, he feels comfortable sharing his vision with Kate. His primary role in our congregation, Disciples United Community Church, is to be a teacher and preacher. Kate, on the other hand, finds energy and creativity in the dynamic process of worship planning, congregational outreach, and teamwork and is the primary pastoral caregiver for our congregation. While Kate preached weekly for a decade at her last congregation, she finds it much more creative to rotate with Bruce in preaching, as they play off one another's insights from week to week.

On a personal note, in terms of our day-to-day relationship, we have worked intentionally to "meet in the middle" between introversion and extroversion, between judging and perceiving personality aspects. After a long day's working, teaching, or consulting, Bruce is ready to read or relax, while Kate is often eager to go out to a movie or with friends. We have found ways to creatively honor our respective personality types by choosing to go out or entertain friends only on "quiet" professional days, when Bruce isn't exhausted by extroversion. We plan our vacations with care to take into consideration our personality types. For instance, contrary to Kate's spontaneous perceiving nature, we plan our beach weeks well in advance. We have agreed that if Kate wants to invite friends to join us for a few days, then ideally they should be fairly introverted or individuated extroverts. Our joyfully "noisy" extroverted friends may join us for a day, but they must be able to understand, and not take offense, if Bruce takes off for an hour's quiet walk on the beach. The holiday environment that we have found most energizing is a learning resort such as the Chautauqua Institution in New York or Ghost Ranch in New Mexico. Such learning resorts combine the arts, educational activities, fellowship, and solitude.

TRANSFORMING TYPES

Throughout this book, we have identified renewed and renewing pastoral vitality and excellence with a commitment to personal growth and creative transformation. While many factors contribute to clergy burnout, a major source of spiritual, emotional, and physical depletion is the perceived inability to change either oneself or one's environment. But, as Viktor Frankl's *Man's Search for Meaning* asserts both in word and deed, the slightest commitment to personal responsibility and creativity can be a matter of life and death, both spiritually and physically. Although we cannot, as Frankl testifies from the vantage point of a German concentration camp, change many of the external circumstances of our lives, we can take responsibility for how we respond to the events of our lives, whether they relate to our health, family life, or congregational situation.[6] Indeed, this text is a sustained call to pastoral vitality through commitment to growing in wisdom and stature as we embrace the fullness of ourselves and God's presence in our lives.

Richard Hamm, former president and general minister of the Christian Church (Disciples of Christ), describes what he calls the "perfect storm" that has rocked mainstream and progressive Christianity over the past thirty years. This constellation of events, which includes the loss of cultural dominance, the movement from the modern to postmodern ethos, the growing obsolescence of denominational structures, inability to respond to generational differences, and a growing sense of fear and anxiety in terms of the future of the church, calls pastoral leaders to radical personal and professional transformation. While once a pastor could focus on excellence in one aspect of pastoral ministry, now he or she must have the flexibility to be visionary, leader, and administrator, amidst a good deal of congregational and cultural chaos. In a time of perpetual whitewater in the church and surrounding culture, effective and healthy pastors must, according to Hamm, go beyond their natural propensities in terms of congregational leadership to embrace other styles of leadership.[7]

In the previous sections, we have suggested that healthy pastoral growth is intimately related to both the awareness of one's own basic personality type and the willingness to embrace the holy otherness of other personality types in yourself, your family, and your congregation. Healthy and vital pastors are persons of stature who mindfully embrace as much of reality as possible, including the fullness of their own personal experience, without losing their personal center and integrity. This process of understanding and embracing otherness, whether in terms of different personality types or parts of ourselves we have neglected, is described by psychologist Carl Jung, the parent of the MBTI, as the journey toward wholeness or individuation.

The journey toward wholeness upon which agile and flexible ministry depends involves claiming and cultivating within ourselves the gifts of other personality types as well as the surprises and resources of the "other" or "shadow" side, the unacknowledged or hidden aspects of ourselves.[8] Put briefly, pastors are called to see God's presence in every personality type, most especially the poles of experience they have de-emphasized or are not their naturally identified preference. The creative spiral of wholeness is energized when we explore and find within ourselves the gifts of introversion and extroversion, intuition and sensing, feeling and thinking, and judging and perceiving. While we still naturally prefer the gifts of particular types, we gain agility and creativity by our ability to move from one pole to the other in our response to the challenges of congregational life and cultural change.

Pastors, of all personality types, heavily modified their sermons and liturgies to respond sensitively to the attacks of September 11, 2001, and to marshal the resources of their congregations to support families in the aftermath of Hurricane Katrina. Today, such responsiveness needs to be a matter of ongoing sensitivity to God's call within the world and our self-awareness and professional growth in understanding our mission as pastors rather than spontaneity. We need to plan for novelty and flexibility. By embracing, to greater or lesser degrees, the gifts of our whole selves, pastors will be able to, in the words of the philosopher Alfred North Whitehead, initiate novelty to match the novelty of their environmental context, whether it be the neighborhood or the nation.

Whether we speak of claiming the power of socially neglected personality types or hidden, and often repressed, aspects of ourselves or others, we believe, with Robert A. Johnson, that to "honor and respect one's own shadow [or holy otherness] is a profound spiritual discipline. It is whole-making and thus holy and the most important experience of a lifetime."[9] Indeed, as Johnson notes, "the religious process," necessary for creative, agile, and nonanxious leadership "consists of restoring the wholeness of the personality."[10] In the spirit of Psalm 139, God's healing work is present in both light and darkness, for "even the darkness is not dark to you; the night is as bright as the day, for darkness is as light to you" (Psa. 139:12). As Jungian psychologist John Sanford proclaims, "God loves your shadow much more than [God] does your [defensive] ego!"[11]

Without going into great detail, our willingness to embrace the holy otherness of ourselves is our greatest asset in appreciating the cultural, personality, and behavioral differences of others. What we reject in ourselves, we often "project" negatively upon others. Our willingness to claim our many-faceted self in all its wonder and challenge is one of the greatest gifts we can give to our congregations, families, relationships, and our own personal health.

While there is no *one* particular path toward individuation or wholeness, we recognize that we can further the process of personal and corporate healthy transformation through seeking to grow in awareness and responsiveness to the diversity in persons and cultures, in gender identity and sexual orientation. We grow in wisdom and stature as we embrace the rich images and themes of our dream life, and the inner images of health and wholeness, peace and justice, in the context of our commitment to spiritual practices that reflect the gifts of our own and other personality types. God's resources for wholeness and leadership are always more than we can imagine, and as we open to the variety of God's gifts in ourselves and others, we will discover the courage and agility to be creative spiritual leaders, visionary thinkers, nonanxious administrators, and creative planners able to navigate the rough waters of cultural and community change.

FEEDING THE MINISTERIAL FIRE

Self-awareness is central to your vital and energetic ministry over the long haul. If you have not previously taken the MBTI, we invite you to take it from a certified Myers-Briggs Personality Type practitioner. Many pastoral counseling centers and spiritual retreat centers have trained professionals or can provide referrals to certified practitioners.

A Holistic Spiritual Practice

In the course of this text, we have lifted up many different spiritual practices as ways of feeding the fire of ministerial and personal life. As you reflect on the spiritual practices you have attempted in the course of reading this book, which practices feel most comfortable to you? Which ones were most difficult to practice? Which ones best fit your personality and way of approaching life?

We encourage you to take time to practice the spiritual activities that are most comfortable for your personality type. Let these practices deepen your unique qualities as God's beloved child.

But also, set aside some time to explore the practices that were most difficult for you. Take time to practice a few of these disciplines as a means of promoting your own personal growth and process of wholeness and individuation. If you struggle with these spiritual practices, consider experimenting with ways to modify them to suit your own personality type or consult with persons who practice or teach these spiritual disciplines. We believe that experimenting with practices characteristic of the "other" side of our lives promotes greater wholeness, maturity, and individuation in our personal and professional lives.

A Practice for Healthy Ministry

Self-awareness finds its fulfillment in the creative integration of contemplation and action in the lives of both introverts and extraverts. As you look at your life in the week ahead, reflect on the following questions:

1. How much quiet time do you need to feel creative and balanced in your life and ministry?

2. Given your personality type, how would you evaluate your current balance of solitude and community, prayer and action, silence and words, and planning in groups and planning in solitude? How might you nurture this balance?

3. What new practices or approaches to life might enhance your personal vitality and sense of calling and bring greater wholeness to your life?

Recognizing the differing styles of spiritual discipline and practical action related to each personality type, take time in the week ahead to seek a healthy balance of action and contemplation, solitude and community. Note how you feel during periods of time when you must live in accordance with the characteristics of another personality type (for example, a contemplative day for an extrovert, a day full of appointments for an introvert, an analytic task for a perceiving type, a day full of unscheduled activities for a judging type, a focus on the big picture theological visions for sensing types, a day with the church budget for a feeling type, an exploration of the emotional nuances of group dynamics for a thinking type, and the challenge of fact-based decision making for an intuitive type). Explore ways to find balance on days in which you must react in the spirit of another personality type.

An Affirmation of Faith

Our own process of personal and professional formation reflects the call and response of God in our lives. As part of the body of Christ, each of us has unique gifts for the transformation and healing of the world as well as our own personal and professional wholeness. Moving within the events of our lives and our unique personal gifts, God affirms that "you are my beloved daughter in whom I am well pleased" or "you are my beloved son in whom I am well pleased." We grow in our own personality type and evolve toward embracing personal wholeness through living by our affirmations:

- God's energy and love flow through my unique personality and giftedness.

- I affirm and honor the unique personality gifts of others.

- I am growing in wisdom and stature as I embrace "holy otherness" in myself and in others.

A Covenant of Wholeness and Vitality

In the weeks ahead, make a covenant with God to grow in your appreciation of your unique personality type and the personality types of others. You may choose these affirmations or ones of your own creation:

- I covenant to grow in self-understanding and healthy embodiment of my unique personality type.

- I covenant to appreciate the holy otherness characteristic of other personality types by responding creatively to their unique gifts.

- I covenant to grow in stature by embracing the totality of my personality, including those positive aspects (my holy otherness) that I most often overlook or deny.

NINE

CHOPPING WOOD, CARRYING WATER

A Zen Buddhist saying notes that "before enlightenment, I chopped wood and carried water; after enlightenment, I chopped wood and carried water." Surely, this saying describes vital, healthy, and creative ministry in the twenty-first century. Vital ministry embraces the whole of a pastor's life, including those simple personal and professional tasks we do day after day. We practice ministry in the same way physicians practice medicine, by mindful awareness of ourselves in body, mind, and spirit and by faithfulness to God in our responses to vulnerable persons, congregational challenges, and cultural changes. Though our work and knowledge is always incomplete and imperfect, we must press on toward the goal of healthy and world-transforming ministry. Energetic and transformative ministry is grounded in intentional actions, practiced over and over, that feed the fire of ministry.

On December 31, 2007, Bruce built a roaring fire in our wood stove not only to create the right atmosphere for writing this final chapter and to warm the main floor of our three-story home, but also to provide a warm welcome to Kate when she awakened. Fires that safely heat and illumine a household are the result of attentiveness to simple details such as chopping and stacking the wood so that it can be easily kindled, and constantly feeding the fire with good, dry wood as well as removing ashes from the fireplace. While there a number of approaches to building and maintaining a fire, depending on the type of wood and fireplace, intentionality and attention are essential if the fire is to provide both heat and light. The same is true for feeding the fires of ministry.

In ministry our goal is never just to avoid burnout, but to promote illumination, warmth, and vitality in all the many practices of ministry. While there is no one path to healthy, creative, and energetic ministry that embraces family life and personal well-being over a lifetime, we have suggested a number of practices of wholeness and vitality that we invite you to embody in your own personal and professional life.

We believe that God is intimately with us, calling us to abundant life in every encounter. God continually supplies our deepest needs in every situation by providing wisdom, insight, energy, endurance, and possibility. Even when our best attempts at personal health and wholeness and ministerial leadership are in jeopardy, nothing can separate us from the lively, uplifting, and healing of love of our ever-present, ever-active God.

We can feed the fire of this divine energy, illuminating and warming our lives, so that it shines brightly through a commitment to practices of:

- Physical and emotional well-being
- Continuing education and theological openness
- Spiritual formation and growth
- Creative and innovative leadership
- Time transformation
- Personal individuation and openness to diversity
- Holistic perspectives on personal and social change

Wherever you are in ministry, you can become a new creation by feeding the fires of your pastoral vitality and wholeness. Even if you are on the edge of burnout or in the midst of brownout, you can rekindle the flame of joyful and enthusiastic ministry that emerged when you first experienced God's call to spiritual leadership in your own life. God is doing a new thing in your life, your congregation, your family, and the world. However hidden from yourself or others, Christ's light is still burning in your heart and mind, awakening you to vital, renewed, and renewing ministry. Feed this ministerial fire! Let God's light shine forth, healing and empowering you, your church, and the world!

NOTES

Acknowledgements

1. For more information on Lancaster Theological Seminary, please consult www.lancasterseminary.edu.

2. For information on Disciples United Community Church, please consult www.ducc.us.

Chapter One

1. Thomas Merton, *The Wisdom of the Desert* (San Francisco: New Directions, 1980), 50.

2. Jackson Carroll, *God's Potters: Pastoral Leadership and the Shaping of Congregations* (Grand Rapids: William B. Eerdmans , 2006), 13.

3. Sandra Bloom, *Creating Sanctuary: Toward the Evolution of Sane Societies* (New York: Routledge, 1997).

4. Anne Wilson Schaef and Diane Fassel, *The Addictive Organization* (San Francisco: HarperSan Francisco, 1988).

5. Marcus Borg, *Meeting Jesus Again for the First Time* (New York: HarperOne, 1995), 32–33.

6. Craig Dykstra, *Growing in the Life of Faith: Education and Christian Practices* (Louisville: Geneva Press, 1999), 69.

7. Brother Lawrence, *Practicing the Presence of God* (Brewster, Mass.: Paraclete Press, 2007).

8. Anthony Robinson, *Leadership for Vital Congregations* (Cleveland: Pilgrim Press, 2007), 115.

9. Dorothy Bass, ed., *Practicing our Faith: A Way of Life for Searching People* (San Francisco: Jossey-Bass, 1999, ix.

10. Thich Nhat Hanh, *Peace Is Every Step* (New York: Bantam, 1992), 10.

11. For more about the transforming power of affirmations, see Bruce Epperly, *The Power of Affirmative Faith* (St. Louis: Chalice Press, 2001), and *Holy Adventure: Forty-One Days of Audacious Living* (Nashville: Upper Room, 2008).

Chapter Two

1. For more on the healings of Jesus, see Bruce Epperly, *God's Touch: Faith, Wholeness, and the Healing Miracles of Jesus* (Louisville: Westminster John Knox, 2001) and *Healing Worship: Purpose and Practice* (Cleveland: Pilgrim Press, 2006); Morton Kelsey, *Healing and Christianity* (Minneapolis: Augsburg, 1995); and Tilda Norberg and Robert Webber, *Stretch Out Your Hand* (Nashville: Upper Room, 1999).

2. Stephanie Paulsell, *Honoring the Body: Meditations on a Christian Practice* (San Francisco: Jossey-Bass, 2003), 89.

3. For more about the Shalem Institute for Spiritual Formation, see www.shalem.org.

4. Paulsell, *Honoring the Body*, 1.

5. Bruce and Katherine Epperly, *Reiki Healing Touch and the Way of Jesus* (Kelowna, B.C: Northstone, 2005).

Chapter Three

1. Bernard Loomer, "S-I-Z-E is the Measure," in James Cargas and Bernard Lee, eds., *Religious Experience and Process Theology* (New York: Paulist Press, 1976), 70.

2. For more on attitudinal healing, see Jerry Jampolsky, *Love Is Letting Go of Fear* (New York: Bantam Books, 1981), and Susan Trout, *To See Differently* (Washington, DC: Three Roses Press, 1990).

3. Bruce Epperly, *The Power of Affirmative Faith* (St. Louis: Chalice Press, 2001).

Chapter Four

1. Susan Cole, Marian Ronan, and Hal Taussig, *Wisdom's Feast: Sophia in Study and Celebration* (New York: Sheed and Ward, 1997), 46.

2. We have substituted the words "awe and reverence" for the word fear in this RSV transation since they best describe the relational aspect of wisdom that lures us to partnership out the experience of love and beauty rather than threat of punishment.

3. While we recommend any of Gerald May's books, we lift up in particular the following: *Addiction and Grace* (New York: HarperOne, 1991); *The Awakened Heart* (San Francisco: HarperSanFrancisco, 1993); *The Dark Night of the Soul* (New York:

HarperOne, 2005). May's four-fold approach to spiritual formation permeates his classic on spirituality and love, *The Awakened Heart*.

4. Elizabeth Barrett Browning (1806–61), "86. From 'Aurora Leigh'," in Nicholson & Lee, eds. *The Oxford Book of English Mystical Verse* (Oxford: Clarendon Press, 1917), xv, 19; Bartleby.com, 2000, www.bartleby.com/236/, accessed July 1, 2008.

5. For more about Oasis Ministries for Spiritual Development, see www.oasismin.org.

6. For more on Jesus' healing ministry, see Bruce Gordon Epperly, *God's Touch: Faith, Wholeness, and the Healing Miracles of Jesus* (Philadelphia: Westminster John Knox Press, 2001) and *Healing Worship: Purpose and Practice* (Cleveland: Pilgrim Press, 2006).

7. Robert Louis Stevenson (1850–94), "The Celestial Surgeon," In *Modern British Poetry*, ed. Louuis Untermeyer (New York: Harcourt, Brace, 1962).

Chapter Five

1. For more about Star Island, see www.starisland.org.

2. Krista Kurth and Suzanne Schmidt, *Running on Plenty at Work: Renewal Strategies for Individuals* (Washington, D.C.: Renewal Resources Press, 2003).

3. Alfred North Whitehead, *Process and Reality: An Essay in Cosmology*, corrected edition, ed. David Ray Griffin and Donald W. Sherburne (New York: Free Press, 1978), 351.

4. For an insightful commentary on the "divine office" and the Rule of St. Benedict, see Norvene Vest, *Preferring Christ* (New York: Morehouse Press, 1997).

5. We have been especially influenced by the work of Phillip Newell, in particular his *Book of Creation: An Introduction to Celtic Spirituality* (Mahweh, N.J.: Paulist Press, 1999). His devotional books, such as *Sounds of the Eternal: A Celtic Psalter* (Grand Rapids: Eerdmans, 2002) and *Celtic Benediction* (Grand Rapids: Eerdmans, 2000) are especially helpful for individual and group morning and evening prayer.

6. Robert Van de Weyer, *Celtic Fire* (New York: Galilee Trade Books, 1991), 79.

7. Ibid., 77.

8. Esther de Waal, *Every Earthly Blessing* (Harrisburg: Morehouse Publishing, 1999), 5.

9. Esther de Waal, *The Celtic Vision* (Ligouri, Mo.: Liguori/Triumph, 2001), 6.

10. Timothy Joyce, *Celtic Quest* (Maryknoll, N.Y.: Orbis Books, 2000), 94.

11. Joyce Rupp describes a coffee and tea spirituality in *The Cup of Our Life* (Notre Dame, Ind.: Ave Maria Press, 1997).

12. Abraham Heschel, *The Sabbath* (New York: Farrar, Straus, and Giroux, 1988), 29.

13. Ibid., 21.

14. Charles E. Hummel, *Freedom from the Tyranny of the Urgent* (Downers Grove, Ill.: InterVarsity Press 1997), 43.

Chapter Six

1. Abraham Joshua Heschel, *The Sabbath* (New York: Farrar, Straus, and Giroux, 1988), 12.

2. The most helpful text in this process was Susan Trout's *To See Differently* (Washington, D.C.: Three Roses Press, 1990).

3. Heidi Neumark, *Breathing Space: A Spiritual Journey in the South Bronx* (Boston: Beacon Press, 2003), 81.

4. For more about reiki healing touch, see Bruce Epperly and Katherine Epperly, *Reiki Healing Touch and the Way of Jesus* (Kelowna, B. C.: Northstone Press, 2006).

5. While there are many fine books on spiritual direction, we recommend Tilden Edwards, *Spiritual Director, Spiritual Companion* (Mahweh, N.J.: Paulist Press, 2001), Margaret Guenther, *Holy Listening: The Art of Spiritual Direction* (Lanham, Md.: Cowley, 1992), and Gerald May, *Care of Mind, Care of Spirit* (San Francisco: HarperOne, 1992).

6. We have discussed pastoral colleague groups through the stages of ministry in Bruce Epperly and Katherine Epperly, *The Four Seasons of Ministry* (Herndon, Va.: Alban Institute, 2008).

7. For more on programs at every season of ministry, see Ibid.

Chapter Seven

1. Chris Hobgood, *Welcoming Resistance* (Herndon, Va.: Alban Institute, 2001), 5.

2. Ibid., 4.

3. For an overview of congregational systems theory, see Peter Steinke, *Congregational Leadership in Anxious Times: Being Calm and Courageous No Matter What Happens* (Herndon, Va.: Alban Institute, 2006), and *How Your Church Family Works: Understanding Congregations as Emotional Systems* (Herndon, Va.: Alban Institute, 2006).

4. We are appreciative of the insights found in Mennonite Conciliation Service, *Mediation and Facilitation Training Manual* (Akron, Pa.: Mennonite Central Committee, 2000), 17–19, and throughout the book.

5. Ibid, 117.

6. Richard Hamm, *Recreating the Church: Leadership for the Postmodern Age* (St. Louis: Chalice Press, 2007), 17.

7. Walter Brueggemann, *Praying the Psalms* (Brockton, Mass.: Cascade Books, 2007) and *The Message of the Psalms: A Theological Commentary* (Minneapolis: Augsburg, 1984).

8. Much of this section is grounded in the insights of Robert Voyle and Kim Voyle, *Core Elements of the Appreciative Way: An Introduction to Appreciative Inquiry for Work and Daily Living* (Hillsboro, Ore.: Clergy Leadership Institute, 2006).

9. Edwin Friedman, *Generation to Generation: Family Process in Church and Synagogue* (New York: Guilford Press, 1985), and Ronald Richardson, *Becoming a Healthier Pastor: Family Systems Theory and the Pastor's Own Family* (Minneapolis: Augsburg, 2005).

10. Bruce and a colleague, Rev. Betty Snapp-Barrett, teach a seminary course in the spirituality of congregational leadership that integrates genogram work, family systems theory, ministerial self-care, spiritual formation, and group process.

11. Sharon Daloz Parks, *Leadership Can Be Taught* (Boston: Harvard University School of Business, 2005).

Chapter Eight

1. While there are many good texts on personality types, much of our work is based on the following texts: David Kiersey and Marilyn Bates, *Please Understand Me II* (New York: Prometheus, 1998); Otto Kroeger and Roy Oswald, *Personality Type and Religious Leadership* (Washington, D.C.: Alban Institute, 1988); Otto Kroeger and Janet Thuesen, *Type Talk: The 16 Personality Types that Determine How We Live, Love, and Work* (New York: Dell, 1988); Isabella Briggs Myers, *Gifts Differing* (Palo Alto: Counseling Psychologists Press, 1980; and, Judith Provost, *Applications of the Myers-Briggs Type Indicator in Counseling* (Palto Alto: Center for the Application of Psychological Type, 1993).

2. For more about Oasis Ministry for Spiritual Development, see www.oasismin.org.

3. Otto Kroeger and Roy Oswald, *Personality Type and Religious Leadership*, 16.

4. Ibid., 22.

5. We refer you to Oswald and Kroeger, *Personality Type and Religious Leadership*, for a comprehensive discussion of personality type constellations and their relationship to the practice of ministry. Put briefly, the basic constellations of type are: ISTJ, ISFJ, INTJ, INFJ, ISTP, ISFP, INFP, INTP, ESTP, ESFP, ENFP, ENTP, ESTJ, ESFJ, ENFJ, ENTJ.

6. Viktor Frankl, *Man's Search for Meaning* (New York: Simon and Schuster, 1959).

7. Richard Hamm, *Recreating the Church: Leadership for a Postmodern Age* (St. Louis: Chalice Press, 2007).

8. We employ the term "other side" or "holy otherness" rather than "shadow" side in order to avoid the implicit racism inherent in privileging "light" or "whiteness" in ministry and psychology.

9. Robert A. Johnson, *Owning Your Own Shadow: Understanding the Dark Side of Your Psyche* (San Francisco: HarperSanFrancisco, 1991), x.

10. Ibid., 9.

11. Ibid., 44.